GOD'S WORD IS FOR YO[U]
AND FOR NOW

OPEN
YOUR
BIBLE

RAECHEL MYERS *and*
AMANDA BIBLE WILLIAMS

SHE
READS
TRUTH

LifeWay Press®
Nashville, Tennessee

The authors are represented by Alive Literary Agency, 7680 Goddard Street, Suite 200, Colorado Springs, CO, 80920. *www.aliveliterary.com*.

ISBN 9781430043317
Item 005757875

Dewey decimal classification: 220.07
Subject headings: BIBLE--STUDY AND TEACHING / GOD / GOSPEL

To order additional copies of this resource, write to LifeWay Church Resources Customer Service; One LifeWay Plaza; Nashville, TN 37234-0113; fax 615.251.5933; phone toll free 800.458.2772; email *orderentry@lifeway.com* or order online at *www.lifeway.com* or visit the LifeWay Christian Store serving you.

Printed in Canada

Adult Ministry Publishing
LifeWay Church Resources
One LifeWay Plaza
Nashville, TN 37234-0152

CONTENTS

ABOUT THE AUTHORS

Raechel Myers loves God's Word. A reluctant writer but lover of story, she delights in the evidence of God's beauty, goodness, and truth in everyday life—just ask her kids. Co-founder and CEO of She Reads Truth, Raechel has a Bachelor's degree in Housing and Environmental Design and is not afraid to paint a whole house over a long weekend. She longs to cook artisanal meals, but loves Chinese takeout, wearing too much chambray, and kissing her husband. Raechel is fueled by double tall mochas and her strong passion to direct women to God and His Word. She lives south of Nashville, Tennessee, with her three favorite people and an old dog named Scout.

Amanda Bible Williams is crazy about words. True words are her favorite, one of many reasons she adores her role as Chief Content Officer of She Reads Truth. Amanda first met Jesus in an East Tennessee church pew as a little girl, and now she finds Him daily in the pages of God's Word and in a loud, old farmhouse east of Nashville where she lives with her husband and three young children. She has degrees in English and Psychology and nearly a Master's in Religion. Amanda enjoys dancing with her kids, reading herself to sleep, and explaining that her maiden name really is Bible.

WHY DO WE OPEN OUR BIBLES?

It's a fair question. After all, we've only just met you and already we're urging you to *Open Your Bible* in big, capital letters. But before you think us too bold (and maybe even a little bossy), can we give you a peek inside our heart for this study?

You see, we used to open our Bibles out of obligation. Perhaps you do too? *Now we open our Bibles because it feels like coming home.*

We used to open our Bibles out of fear. Maybe you know the feeling? Now we open our Bibles for a fresh breath of the truest freedom we've ever known.

We used to open our Bibles to find ourselves. Now we open our Bibles to find our God.

Hear the happy desperation in our voices when we admit to you: *We open our Bibles because we just can't not.* We open our Bibles because God's Word is living and active, given to us for our salvation and sanctification, for our comfort and joy. We open our Bibles because Jesus, the Living Word in the flesh, is there in its pages—because "God's love was revealed among us in this way: God sent His One and Only Son into the world so that we might *live* through Him" (1 John 4:9).

We open our Bibles not just because we *feel* lost, but because without Him we truly *are* lost. We open our Bibles

because we need the good news of the gospel—not just on Sundays, but every day.

Every day we need the gospel and every day the gospel is true.

To quote Tim Keller, the true gospel is this: *"We are more sinful and flawed in ourselves than we ever dared believe, yet at the very same time we are more loved and accepted in Jesus Christ than we ever dared hope."* [1]

Friends, the gospel of Jesus Christ is the reason we open our Bibles. Jesus is the Living Word, revealed in the black and white truths of Scripture.

We are so glad you're here! We are humbled and thankful for the privilege of sitting down with you via the pages of this book (that will one day fade away) to point you to THE Book (that will endure forever!) and remind you of these glorious truths:

The Bible is for you and it is for now.

But it is not about you—it is about God! It is about His steadfast love for His people. It is about His sovereign plan, His grace, and His glory, and you are meant to read it.

No matter where you are, find Him when you open your Bible.

OPEN

YOUR

BIBLE

"I just can't open my Bible."

They were only asking for prayer requests, but I was surrounded by people who loved me and it felt safe enough to just be honest. It had been four months since we buried our stillborn daughter, and just as many since my aching arms had reached for my Bible. My very wounded heart—which lived and breathed and clung to the Book like never before throughout the uncertainty of my pregnancy—felt betrayed, weak, and hopeless.

There I sat in Tara's living room with a dozen other women, circled up for the first Bible study I'd attended since our Evie Grace was born. I really only came because I needed to get out of the house.

My soul was weary.

No one gasped at my words. No one troubleshot. Instead of judgment, even instead of a "You've just got to do it!", my very blonde and very quiet friend Allison opened the worn pages of the Bible in her lap and simply said, "That's okay. Let me read it to you instead."

Lifting her bookmark from its place, she began to read Psalm 62. "For God alone my soul waits in silence; from him comes my salvation. He only is my rock and my salvation, my fortress; I shall not be greatly shaken..."

As she read on through the end of the chapter, these friends of mine gathered closer. When Allison finished, Kari began to read from her Bible, then Holly, then Danielle. Like I was a person starving, too weak to lift food to my own mouth, they spoon-fed Scripture while I sat and wept and listened to the Word that never stopped being alive or true, even when it remained unread and unopened.

What has kept you from opening your Bible?

Maybe your heart has been wounded like mine, and the very words that have the power to comfort and restore remind you instead of what you've lost.

Perhaps it's not like that at all. Maybe you're afraid of what you'll find. *Will it be convicting? Will it be hard to understand? What if I open my Bible to find the truth is too hard to bear?*

It's possible you haven't opened your Bible lately—or ever—because it's not important. You may believe it's true and good for others, but it doesn't seem necessary for you. Or perhaps you have the basics down and don't feel a need to dig deeper.

Maybe it *is* important to you, but it's just not *urgent*. You think the Bible is definitely worth reading and would love to make some time to sit down and read it, but there is always something more urgent that needs to be done, so your Bible remains closed.

Maybe you feel downright disqualified or unequipped. You suspect the Bible isn't for *you*—it's for pastors and theologians, too difficult to navigate independently. You've tried to open it and read it on your own, but quickly found it was more complicated than you expected.

But here's the thing—

The Bible is for you, and it is for right now. It's for you if you've never read it, and it's for you if you have seventeen doctorates in theology. (Anyone?) It's for the moment you are so overcome with grief that your body forgets to breathe in and out on its own, and it's for the time you really don't have time to open its pages for yourself.

We do not have to be biblical scholars to read this Book. You, right where you are, do not have to wait for someone to take you by the hand to open the pages of Scripture. You can open your Bible just as you are.

Move forward in this study knowing you are not disqualified. No amount of knowledge or accomplishments makes you more or less able to meet God in His Word. **Nothing you are doing, have done, or will do renders you ineligible for the good news of the gospel.**

All the things you imagine you've done wrong when it comes to your "quiet time"? The lostness you feel when you consider opening The Book of All Books for the very first time? Let them go. Understand here and now that yes, this Book is holy and it is sacred and good. But this Book exists for moments just like this—the moment you lay it open and look for *Him*.

WELCOME!

Before every group time, take a moment to read the "Start Here" to prepare for the discussion.

As we begin, discuss the following questions with your group:

What drew you to this study?

What words would you use to describe your relationship with God's Word?

How confident are you in studying God's Word? Why?

Share with the group something you hope to learn from this study.

WATCH THE VIDEO:

To hear more from Raechel and Amanda, download the optional video bundle to view Week One at *www.lifeway.com/openyourbible*.

NOW, LET'S TALK:

Why haven't you opened your Bible?

Imagine an empty room, yourself in one corner and your Bible in the other. You long to connect with God's Word in a meaningful way! But as you pick up your foot to move forward, walls emerge from the floor, blocking you from your destination.

> *What are those walls? Are they physical, emotional, circumstantial, spiritual? Can you name them? What in your heart or life keeps you from getting closer?*

> *Share your walls with the group. Do you have any walls in common? What are they?*

> *What happens if we don't open our Bibles?*

WHEN WE DON'T OPEN OUR BIBLES, WE MISS OUT ON THE BENEFITS OF GOD'S WORD.

> **Read the following verses from Psalm 119 together and discuss the specific benefits of reading Scripture.**

PSALM 119:98

> *It gives _____.*

PSALM 119:107

> *It gives _____.*

PSALM 119:130

> *It gives _____.*

PSALM 119:147

> *It gives _____.*

PSALM 119:165

> *It gives _____.*

WHEN WE DON'T OPEN OUR BIBLES, WE MISS OUT ON THE FULLNESS OF THE SHEPHERD'S PRESENCE.

Read these verses from Psalm 23 together and discuss the effects of remaining in the Lord's presence.

PSALM 23:1

He gives _____.

PSALM 23:2-3A

He gives _____.

PSALM 23:3B

He gives _____.

PSALM 23:4

He gives _____.

PSALM 23:5

He gives _____.

PSALM 23:6

He pursues us in _____.

WHEN WE DON'T OPEN OUR BIBLES, IT DOES NOT CHANGE WHO GOD IS.

Malachi 3:6 says, "For I am the LORD, I do not change" (NKJV). God is immutable, unchangeable.

OPEN YOUR BIBLE AND READ THE FOLLOWING VERSES. AFTER EACH VERSE, IDENTIFY ONE UNCHANGING ATTRIBUTE* OF GOD THAT WE ENCOUNTER IN THE PAGES OF SCRIPTURE.

ATTRIBUTES OF GOD	SCRIPTURE	TEXT
	1 Samuel 2:2	There is no one holy like the LORD.
	Psalm 25:8	The LORD is good and upright.
	Psalm 86:5	For You, Lord, are kind and ready to forgive, rich in faithful love to all who call on You.
	Psalm 115:3	Our God is in heaven and does whatever He pleases.
	Psalm 116: 5	The LORD is gracious and righteous; our God is compassionate.
	Psalm 145:17	The LORD is righteous in all His ways and gracious in all His acts.
	Isaiah 55:8-9	"For My thoughts are not your thoughts, and your ways are not My ways." This is the LORD's declaration. "For as heaven is higher than earth, so My ways are higher than your ways, and My thoughts than your thoughts."
	Acts 17:27-28	He did this so they might seek God, and perhaps they might reach out and find Him, though He is not far from each one of us. For in Him we live and move and exist, as even some of your own poets have said, "For we are also His offspring."

ATTRIBUTES OF GOD	SCRIPTURE	TEXT
	Hebrews 4:13	No creature is hidden from Him, but all things are naked and exposed to the eyes of Him to whom we must give an account.
	Hebrews 13:8	Jesus Christ is the same yesterday, today, and forever.
	James 1:17	Every generous act and every perfect gift is from above, coming down from the Father of lights; with Him there is no variation or shadow cast by turning.
	1 John 3:20, NKJV	For if our heart condemns us, God is greater than our heart, and knows all things.
	1 John 4:8	The one who does not love does not know God, because God is love.

OPEN YOUR BIBLE AND READ THE FOLLOWING VERSES ABOUT GOD'S FAITHFUL LOVE. NOTICE THE DEFINITIVE WORDS IN BOLD BELOW.

ROMANS 5:8

*But God **proves** His own love for us in that while we were still sinners, Christ died for us!*

ROMANS 8:38-39, ESV

*For I am **sure** that neither death nor life, nor angels nor rulers, nor things present nor things to come, nor powers, nor height nor depth, nor anything else in all creation, will be able to separate us from the love of God in Christ Jesus our Lord.*

1 JOHN 4:16, NIV

*And so we **know** and **rely** on the love God has for us. God is love.*

WHAT HAPPENS IF WE DO OPEN OUR BIBLES?

Like Raechel's friends did for her, take turns reading the Scriptures below aloud to one another. Before you read each passage, look each other in the eye and say out loud, "This is for you and this is for now."

Will this be awkward? Yes! Will it be worth it? Absolutely! The Word of God is TRUE. It is living and active. What a privilege to speak God's Word to one another!

OPEN YOUR BIBLE AND READ THESE PASSAGES TO ONE ANOTHER.

PSALM 62:5-8

ISAIAH 53:5

ZEPHANIAH 3:17

2 PETER 3:8-9

FOR DEEPER STUDY,
ANSWER THE FOLLOWING QUESTIONS ABOUT EACH PASSAGE:

- *How is this passage about God? What does it say about Him?*
- *How is this passage for you and for now?*

HAVE ONE PERSON IN YOUR GROUP PRAY THIS PRAYER ALOUD.

> *Jesus, we are hungry for Your Word, but we don't always know where to begin.*
>
> *Will You help us?*
>
> *Father, we come to You confessing our inadequacy.*
>
> *We need Your grace.*
>
> *Holy Spirit, be our comfort and our guide.*
>
> *Draw us into the pages of Scripture and reveal Yourself to us there.*
>
> *Give us hearts that desire to open our Bibles.*
>
> *Amen.*

Even when you don't open your Bible, God's love for you doesn't change.

I can't make
the Bible come alive...
the Bible is already
alive. it makes
me come alive.
R.C. SPROUL

DAY ONE
THE BIBLE IS TRUE

"What is truth?"

This is the question Pilate asks Jesus, bound-up and bloodied, as He stands trial outside the governor's headquarters. It's the question we've all asked at various times in our lives. Somehow, as hard as it can be to spot a lie, it's even more difficult to discern what is true.

As Pilate meets with Jesus' accusers on that Good Friday, truth seems to be the question of the day.

OPEN YOUR BIBLE TO JOHN 18:28-40 AND READ JOHN'S FULL ACCOUNT OF JESUS BEFORE PILATE. CIRCLE PILATE'S QUESTION IN VERSE 38.

When Pilate asks what charge they bring against Jesus, His accusers reason a twisted-up response: "If this man weren't a criminal, we wouldn't have handed Him over to you."

So Pilate tells them, "Take Him yourselves and judge Him according to your law."

But they can't. Because their law won't allow them to put Him to death. So Pilate relents to their demands and presses Jesus further. "Are You the King of the Jews?"

"My kingdom is not of this world," Jesus replies.

"You are a king then?" Pilate asks.

"You say that I'm a king," Jesus replies. "I was born for this, and I have come into the world for this: to testify to the truth. Everyone who is of the truth listens to My voice."

Pilate's response still echoes through the ages: "What is truth?" And with that, the Roman governor of Judea left it to the crowd to decide the fate of his prisoner.

We want to wag our fingers at Pilate for being blind to the Truth standing right in front of His face. How could he have missed the Word made flesh being led like a lamb to the slaughter on the doorstep of his own home?

Discerning the truth is sometimes harder than we expect. When was the last time you struggled to discern the truth? When have you wished you didn't recognize the truth because of the way it convicted you? I wonder if that's how Pilate felt.

Jesus knew the answer to Pilate's question before he asked it. God's Word is truth.

In the garden hours earlier, before His arrest, Jesus prayed to the Father for His disciples, "Sanctify them by the truth; Your word is truth" (John 17:17). Jesus knew full well what these four words—"Your word is truth"— meant. He knew what was coming next would be the making-true of centuries of Old Testament prophecies. Mankind was under a curse and in a debt of sin so deep their only payment could be death—His or theirs.

Not only did Jesus know the truth, He was prepared to give His life for it.

Friends, whatever we read in the rest of this study is meaningless if we don't believe the Bible is true. The Law given to Moses and fulfilled in Christ, the good news of the gospel, the promises upon which our hope is built—it is either all true or not true at all. Truth isn't about expediency and it's not about comfort. There aren't degrees of truth. Because the Bible is true, even the parts we don't understand are good news!

WHAT DOES THE BIBLE SAY ABOUT ITSELF?

OPEN YOUR BIBLE TO EACH PASSAGE BELOW AND JOURNAL ABOUT WHAT THESE VERSES SAY ABOUT SCRIPTURE.

1 KINGS 8:56

PSALM 119:89

PSALM 119:151

PSALM 119:160

2 TIMOTHY 3:16-17

HEBREWS 1:1-2

1 PETER 1:25

2 PETER 1:16-21

Opening your Bible won't always be easy. But, by God's good grace, the more you open your Bible, the more sure you will become of its truth. Whether opening God's Word for the first time or five hundredth, let's stake our collective flag in the ground of Jesus' words in John 17:17: *Your word is truth.*

THE BIBLE IS COMPLETE

I'm a word nerd through and through.

My college roommate and I used to proofread the church bulletin for our own amusement, sharing good-natured belly laughs over punctuation mishaps. I find as much joy in a good string of words as I do a twinkling string of Christmas lights. I google puzzling plurals for fun, and I've legitimately lost sleep over English language conundrums most people couldn't care less about. I can't help it—I'm passionate about words and the way we use them. Correct grammar ministers to my heart.

Words are one way God reveals Himself to us, but they aren't the only way.

OPEN YOUR BIBLE AND READ PSALM 19:1-6. LIST THE WAYS THE WORLD AROUND US PROCLAIMS GOD'S TRUTH. LOOK ESPECIALLY FOR THE ACTION VERBS AND DESCRIPTIVE WORDS AND PHRASES USED.

In His love and mercy, the infinite God of the universe freely reveals Himself to His creation *by* His creation. Theologians call this God's "general revelation." It's what we learn about the existence and majesty of God when we see the sun rise over the bay, notice the flight pattern of an endless string of migrating birds, or find a brightly-colored bloom where a green bud used to be.

Stunning as these revelatory sights are, they're not even the best part. God's gracious revelation of Himself continues in the words of Scripture and the person of Jesus Christ. The Bible is God's "special revelation" to us.

OPEN YOUR BIBLE AND READ PSALM 19:7-11. IDENTIFY THE CHARACTERISTICS AND RESULTS OF GOD'S WORD. IN YOUR BIBLE OR IN THE PASSAGE BELOW, CIRCLE THE CHARACTERISTICS AND UNDERLINE THE RESULTS.

PSALM 19:7-11

7 The instruction of the LORD is perfect,
renewing one's life;
the testimony of the LORD is trustworthy,
making the inexperienced wise.
8 The precepts of the LORD are right,
making the heart glad;
the command of the LORD is radiant,
making the eyes light up.
9 The fear of the LORD is pure,
enduring forever;
the ordinances of the LORD are reliable
and altogether righteous.
10 They are more desirable than gold—
than an abundance of pure gold;
and sweeter than honey,
which comes from the honeycomb.
11 In addition, Your servant is warned by them;
there is great reward in keeping them.

From the grandest story to the smallest sentence, Scripture says all God intends for it to say—not more, not less. We can trust it down to the letter.

The Word of God is about God and it is whole.

The Pharisees touted their strict adherence to Scripture. They also spent a lot of time accusing Jesus of the opposite, claiming He disrespected and even opposed Scripture. Take a look at what Jesus said during the Sermon on the Mount as He defended Himself against these claims:

Don't assume that I came to destroy the Law or the Prophets. **I did not come to destroy but to fulfill.** *For I assure you: Until heaven and earth pass away, not the smallest letter or one stroke of a letter will pass from the law until all things are accomplished (Matt. 5:17-18, emphasis added).*

Even the most minute parts of the Law mattered to Jesus. That "smallest letter" He mentioned? At the time, it was the *iota* in the Greek alphabet and the *yod* in the Hebrew. The yod is about the size of our apostrophe—a speck on the page, yet a promise not forgotten by our great God! Jesus vowed that none of the Law, not even a yod, will go forgotten or unfulfilled. (That makes this Oxford comma-loving girl raise her praise hands high!)

If the Law were indeed a to-do list as the Pharisees believed—and as we are daily tempted to believe—then the checklist would never end. We couldn't do it. But in Christ, every last item is checked off as done! When Jesus breathed "It is finished" from the cross, He meant it (John 19:30).

God's Word is given to us complete, and it is completely fulfilled in the life and person of Jesus.

Friends, hear this sweet promise. The Holy Bible we open today is not lacking—not then, not now, not ever. It is not unfinished or ineffective, and there is nothing we can do to make it more complete. Scripture was purposefully created, divinely inspired, and given for us by God Himself. Everything we need to know about the God who formed us, who loves us, who pursues us and rescues us from the pit is found in the pages of His Book.

I love the matter-of-factness with which author and theologian Kevin DeYoung describes the fullness of God's Word:

You do not need another special revelation from God outside the Bible. You can listen to the voice of God every day. Christ still speaks, because the Spirit has already spoken. If you want to hear from God, go to the book that records only what he has said. Immerse yourself in the word of God. You will not find anything more sure.[1]

God's Word is complete. It is complete not only because it has no missing parts, no inadvertently omitted truths, no unintended gaps, but because it has been accomplished to the letter—even the tiniest letter—by our Savior.

OPEN YOUR BIBLE TO PSALM 119:89. WRITE A SHORT PRAYER ASKING GOD TO GIVE YOU FAITH TO BELIEVE THE WORDS OF THIS VERSE, TO SEE AND RECEIVE GOD'S WORD AS TRUE AND COMPLETE.

THE BIBLE IS LIVING AND ACTIVE

My grandma has the coolest morning ritual.

It begins with quiet—the kind of quiet she'll freely admit was much harder to come by when she was raising five boys. She opens her Bible and reads from it first thing. When she's finished, she presses back in her recliner, drapes a cloth over her face to prevent distractions, then proceeds to pray for each of her five sons, each of their wives, and all 17 of her grandchildren, their spouses, and their children. Each of us by name. Every morning.

I love this so much.

My grandma (her name is Marvolene!) has loved Jesus for three quarters of a century. She knows the Bible well, yet even at a glorious 80 years old, it is still her daily destination for fresh interaction with her Savior.

I don't see Grandma Marvolene very often. She and Grandpa live in Michigan and we're in Tennessee. But, I had the opportunity to make a trip to visit them recently and I'll never forget the sweetness of that time.

Grandma and I sat together in her living room while my husband and kids took a tractor ride in the yard with Grandpa. She didn't waste time. The moment she had the chance, she leaned in to tell me what the Lord had been teaching her in His Word.

Just a few days earlier the Lord had brought a line of Scripture to her mind: *"And as they went, they were cleansed."* She must have read it before, but she couldn't quite place it. After a little hunting, she found the words in Luke 17 (NKJV).

Smiling through tears, Grandma shared what new thing she was learning in the Word in this season. She wanted to read the story to me but her eyes were a little too teary to see, so I reached for her Bible and read it aloud for the both of us. Just me and my grandma, her Bible open in front of us, studying God's Word together.

OPEN YOUR BIBLE TO LUKE 17:11-19 AND READ THE STORY OF THE TEN LEPERS FOR YOURSELF. THE WORDS GRANDMA'S HEART REMEMBERED WERE IN VERSE 14.

Did Jesus heal the ten lepers immediately? What did he tell them to do?

When were the lepers healed?

My sweet grandma is facing the greatest medical battle of her life and these words have been an immense comfort to her. But, by remembering this passage at such a relatable time, do you think she took it as a promise that she will be healed like the lepers? No. She knows the promises of the Bible are even better than that. However, understanding Luke 17 as a historical account of one of Christ's miracles, she was reminded of two important truths about her Jesus:

1. JESUS TAKES NOTICE OF THE HURTING.

2. HE ASKS US TO OBEY IN FAITH, TRUSTING THAT HE IS SOVEREIGN OVER OUR BODIES.

We talked and wept and prayed as a family that afternoon. We thanked the Father for taking notice of Grandma Marvolene's pain. We asked the Holy Spirit to help us obey in faith as we trust our lives to our Maker. And as we said "goodbye until next time," I was buoyed in my understanding of how "living and active" God's Word truly is.

OPEN YOUR BIBLE TO HEBREWS 4:12 AND COPY THE FULL VERSE BELOW. CIRCLE THE TWO ADJECTIVES USED TO DESCRIBE GOD'S WORD.

For now let's focus on the truth in the first half of this verse. What does it mean for God's Word to be "living" and "active"?

GOD'S WORD IS LIVING.

OPEN YOUR BIBLE TO THE PASSAGES BELOW. MATTHEW HENRY SAYS, "SAINTS DIE, AND SINNERS DIE; BUT THE WORD OF GOD LIVES."[2] WRITE A STATEMENT ABOUT GOD'S WORD UNDER EACH REFERENCE.

ISAIAH 40:8

"The grass withers, the flowers fade, but the word of our God remains forever."

ZECHARIAH 1:5-6

"Where are your ancestors now? And do the prophets live forever? But didn't My words and My statutes that I commanded My servants the prophets overtake your ancestors? They repented and said: As the LORD of Hosts purposed to deal with us for our ways and deeds, so He has dealt with us."

2 TIMOTHY 2:9

I suffer for it to the point of being bound like a criminal, but God's message is not bound.

GOD'S WORD IS ACTIVE.

OPEN YOUR BIBLE TO DEUTERONOMY 32:46-47.

What does Moses say about God's words that came to the Israelites in the wilderness?

ISAIAH 55:10-11

> *10 For just as rain and snow fall from heaven*
>
> *and do not return there*
>
> *without saturating the earth*
>
> *and making it germinate and sprout,*
>
> *and providing seed to sow*
>
> *and food to eat,*
>
> *11 so My word that comes from My mouth*
>
> *will not return to Me empty,*
>
> *but it will accomplish what I please*
>
> *and will prosper in what I send it to do.*

God's Word does something, doesn't it? The prophet Isaiah tells us God's Word is like the rain and snow causing things to sprout. It brings forth life!

How has God's Word watered your life? How have you seen the Word of the Lord not return empty in your life or someone else's life?

What makes this possible? Why do you think Grandma Marvolene remembered the passage she did at the time she did?

Grandma Marvolene has been studying Scripture for 75 years. The Holy Spirit guides us too, even in our immaturity—especially in our immaturity!—to remember and understand the truths of Scripture. Jesus left us the Spirit as our guide to illuminate what He has already inspired!

Based on John's words in 1 John 2:27, is it possible for a person to sit down by herself and be taught the truth from God's Word?

According to John 14:26, what does Jesus promise the Holy Spirit will do?

Write a prayer of thanks to God for His living and active Word. Ask the Holy Spirit to guide you as you read, illuminating what He has already inspired.

THE BIBLE IS ENOUGH

Sometimes I doubt the gospel is enough for me.

The rest of you, sure, but not me. It is a "too good to be true" situation and I'm the unlucky gal who falls outside redemption's lines.

These are the lies the Enemy tells me—lies that can only be quieted by the resounding truth of God's Word. Take these words from Romans 11:6 for example: "But if it is by grace, it is no longer on the basis of works; otherwise grace would no longer be grace" (ESV). **God's Word is the only light bright enough to drown the darkness of my doubt.**

Even still, when I hear the words "The Bible is enough," my cynicism kicks into high gear.

How can the Bible be enough when the brokenness of this world is so vast and the consequences so painful? Does saying "The Bible is enough" mean it is the solution to all our problems? Does it mean that, in light of eternity, our problems don't exist or matter? Is the Bible the Sunday School answer to every earthly ache?

It's easy to see how we who call ourselves believers can once again—and regularly—become doubters.

So what are we saying when we say the Bible is enough?

To say God's Word is enough is not to say our need is not real or great. It is not to diminish the struggles of our circumstances or dismiss the validity of our pain. The opposite is true! **To say God's Word is enough is to acknowledge our need as *so great*, our pain and problems *so real*, that only God's Word and the Living Word—Jesus—can bring real redemption.**

Great! But what does that look like exactly?

To bring this concept to life, let's head over to the Old Testament and read the story of God's provision for His people as they wandered for decades in the wilderness.

Now, look back at verse 4, and jot down the answers to these questions:

Where did the bread come from?

How often were the people to gather it?

How much were they instructed to gather?

The bread that rained from heaven was exactly proportionate to the Israelites' individual and immediate needs. In the same way, God's Word is enough for you and for me—each and every time we read it. We are freed from the panic of opening our Bibles and wondering, *What if it isn't true? What if it isn't enough?* God's Word is so supremely sufficient that hoarding is not just unnecessary, it's silly!

The Bible is God's provision for us. It is enough today and it will be enough when we come back to gather more tomorrow. We can consume it without fear of diminishing God's goodness, using up His truth, squeezing out the last drop of His mercy. The famous 19th century preacher Charles Spurgeon may have said it best: "If Christ were only a cistern, we might soon exhaust his fullness, but who can drain a fountain?"[3]

God's Word is enough because the One who gives it is infinitely enough. He is the source of all truth, and He is inexhaustible.

Did the Israelites obey God's command to gather only the manna needed for the day?

Why do you think they struggled with this instruction?

The Israelites doubted that God's provision was truly enough for their survival. Have you ever experienced similar doubt when it comes to whether God's Word is truly enough for you? Why or why not?

Just after feeding the five thousand and walking on water, Jesus described Himself to His disciples this way:

JOHN 6:48-51

I am the bread of life. Your fathers ate the manna in the wilderness, and they died. This is the bread that comes down from heaven so that anyone may eat of it and not die. I am the living bread that came down from heaven. If anyone eats of this bread he will live forever. The bread that I will give for the life of the world is My flesh.

Jesus, the Living Word, looked His disciples in the eyes and said, *I am enough.* It was a bold claim, one that many of those following Him doubted. Verse 66 tells us some turned away right then and there, prompting Jesus to ask, "What about you? Are you going to walk away, too?" (John 6:67, my paraphrase).

I love Simon Peter's response to Jesus—a heaping helping of faith with a generous side of holy fear: "Lord, to whom shall we go? You have the words of eternal life" (John 6:68, ESV).

Indeed, friends, where *would* we go? Only to God.

Only His Word can fill us up. Only His Word meets us at the precise intersection of our need and His provision. Like the bread that fell from the sky to feed God's people in the wilderness, we must receive and take in God's Word as our daily bread, our perfectly portioned manna for the day.

It is sufficient and true, it is for us and for now—and it is enough.

OPEN YOUR BIBLE AND READ ISAIAH 55:1-3.

> *Read it again, this time aloud, and hear the Lord's gracious invitation to you.*
>
> *Write the first half of verse 3 below, noticing the urgency of the words.*

WEEK 2

APPROACH
TRUTH

I have always loved climbing trees.

When I was a little girl in Michigan, we lived near the edge of town, in a white Victorian with a great big backyard. In the far corner, beyond the sandbox and past the swing set, stood an enormous tree with a thousand sturdy branches. I'm sure the tree wasn't as big as it felt to five-year-old me, but from where I found myself most days, lounging in its lower limbs, I was pretty sure I could climb up and up and up in that tree forever. It was old but solid, and it beckoned me further up with each visit.

I trusted that tree. Even when I was young and the tree was oh-so big, I didn't let my smallness keep me away. I simply started right where I was, taking it a branch at a time. Slowly but surely I became confident in myself as a climber, and I found I could rely on the tree to hold me. I had a relationship with the tree—a relationship built on trust.

As believers, I think our hesitation to approach God's Word with confidence comes down to a question of trust:

CAN I TRUST THE BIBLE AS SURE FOOTING FOR EVEN MY UNCERTAIN FEET?

I hear you, friends. I absolutely find myself feeling less than equipped when I approach my Bible most days. I also see you hesitantly leaning in, wondering what I may have to say about the reliability of God's Word. That's great—lean on in!

When I recall my five-year-old approach to that great big climbing tree, I think of a new believer's approach to the Bible. Although someone bigger and stronger may have been able to enjoy the full height and glory that tree had to offer, at age five, I was appropriately challenged and completely satisfied with the branches within my reach.

That tree was for me, just as much as it was for someone twice my age.
Waiting to explore its branches until I felt I was "enough" would have meant missing the joy and exercise of approaching it at my current capacity.

My childhood climbing tree, with its deep, wide root system and its branches so thick and artfully woven they were almost a hammock of limbs, proved reliable and trustworthy. Exploring that tree, like approaching the pages of God's Holy Word, was challenging yet delightful. It did not fail me. And, sisters, God's Word will not fail you.

LOOKING BACK:

In Day Four last week, we read about the Israelites collecting their "perfectly portioned" manna every day. Did that change the way you "gather" Scripture as daily bread? How so?

Sometimes we're tempted to forego personal Bible reading. Is that a struggle for any of you? Why?

Last week we learned that the Bible is for *now*. But now we are learning the Bible is for *you*. Have you ever felt disqualified to approach God's Word? If so, why? Talk about what it means to understand that the Bible is intended specifically for you.

WATCH THE VIDEO:

To hear more from Raechel and Amanda, download the optional video bundle to view Week Two at *www.lifeway.com/openyourbible.*

NOW, LET'S TALK:

What was your family's attitude toward God's Word when you were growing up?

Were Bibles present in your home? If so, how were they treated? Have the Bibles in your life generally been open or closed?

Have you ever felt like you weren't "big enough" or "strong enough" to approach the Bible on your own?

Whether you question the Bible's trustworthiness or your own worthiness, climb on with confidence! In its pages you will find:

THE BIBLE IS TRUSTWORTHY.

Like a healthy tree with deep roots and wide branches, the Bible and all its promises can be trusted.

Are there promises God has made in His Word that you sometimes struggle to believe? Discuss some of those as a group, then read the verses below, encouraging one another that the Bible is trustworthy.

OPEN YOUR BIBLE AND READ THESE VERSES ALOUD.

JOSHUA 21:45, ESV

Not one word of all the good promises that the LORD had made to the house of Israel had failed; all came to pass.

2 SAMUEL 7:28, ESV

And now, O Lord GOD, you are God, and your words are true, and you have promised this good thing to your servant.

PSALM 19:7, ESV

The law of the LORD is perfect, reviving the soul; the testimony of the LORD is sure, making wise the simple.

PROVERBS 30:5, ESV

Every word of God proves true.

LUKE 21:33

Heaven and earth will pass away, but My words will never pass away.

THE BIBLE IS FOR YOU AND FOR NOW.

Don't waste time waiting to be "big enough" or wise enough. God's Word is living and active and relevant for *you* today.

OPEN YOUR BIBLE AND READ THESE VERSES ALOUD.

MARK 2:16-17

2 CORINTHIANS 12:9

How do these passages show us in different ways that God's Word is for you and for now?

Refer back to the Week Two "Start Here." If our aim is to grow in wisdom and understanding of God's Word in those high-up branches, where must every climber begin?

Like that strong, expansive tree, the Bible welcomes and challenges both new believers and life-long climbers. What has that looked like in your life? Where in the tree are you today?

As we go home from our time together this week, let's take four days to dig deeper into what it means to approach God's Word reverently, confidently, regularly, and prayerfully.

God's Word is approachable, and it should be approached every day.

Whatever else
in the Bible catches your
eye, do not let it
distract you from
Him. J.I. PACKER

DAY ONE
APPROACH TRUTH REVERENTLY

"You're driving a deadly weapon."

My new driver's license was still warm from the lamination machine as we pulled away from the DMV on my sixteenth birthday, and my dad was not mincing words. Driving a car was a big deal to me—it meant freedom! It was a big deal to him, too—he hoped I understood the power I had just been given, not simply over my own life, but all those who shared the road with me.

We learn from an early age not to run with scissors, to always cap permanent markers, and to look both ways before we cross the street. Scissors, markers, and streets were all awesome tools for daily kid-life, but if they weren't handled with care, the results could be disastrous.

Thankfully, as we grow older, not injuring ourselves with scissors requires less concentration than before. Instead, we're learning how to dice veggies with a chef's knife, how to wield power tools and credit cards, and how words can build or break a person. The more powerful a thing is, the more it demands our respect.

Outside of God Himself, nothing is more powerful than God's Word. And so, nothing is more deserving of our respect and reverence than the Bible! It is more powerful than any knife or car or uncapped Sharpie® could ever be. But do we treat it that way?

Take a moment to consider the word "reverence." Google tells me reverence is "a feeling or attitude of deep respect tinged with awe."[1] Does that describe how I approach Scripture?

Make a short list of some things that make you feel deep respect or awe. (I think of the time I flew over the Grand Canyon in an airplane, the first time I saw the Atlantic Ocean, and the moment I saw my newborn son's face!)

Do you feel this way when you approach the Bible? Do you want to?

The psalmist is talking about how magnificent or majestic the Lord is (depending on your Bible's translation).

In verses 1 and 9, underline what David specifically says is magnificent.

PSALM 8

1 Yahweh, our Lord,

how magnificent is Your name throughout the earth!

You have covered the heavens with Your majesty.

2 Because of Your adversaries,

You have established a stronghold

from the mouths of children and nursing infants

to silence the enemy and the avenger.

3 When I observe Your heavens,

the work of Your fingers,

the moon and the stars,

which You set in place,

4 what is man that You remember him,

the son of man that You look after him?

5 You made him little less than God

and crowned him with glory and honor.

6 You made him lord over the works of Your hands;

You put everything under his feet:

7 all the sheep and oxen,

as well as the animals in the wild,

8 the birds of the sky,

and the fish of the sea

that pass through the currents of the seas.

9 Yahweh, our Lord,

how magnificent is Your name throughout the earth!

What else does the Bible say about God's name?

EXODUS 20:7

DEUTERONOMY 12:11

1 SAMUEL 12:22

PROVERBS 18:10

ROMANS 10:13

The Bible is not unclear about the power of God's name. It is powerful enough to save us and able to protect us.

His name and His Word are His revelations to us of who our mysterious, sovereign, loving, and holy Maker is. Everything about God must be approached with reverence (or "deep respect, tinged with awe").

To what is God's Word compared, and what is it able to accomplish?

And in Ephesians 6:17, what does Paul call God's Word?

Just like a real-life sword, the Bible has power to cut to the heart. And unlike a real-life sword, it is mysteriously and wonderfully able to pierce our most secret thoughts and intentions, like Simeon prophesied Jesus would do:

LUKE 2:35

> *And a sword will pierce your own soul—that the thoughts of many hearts may be revealed.*

The Bible is a life-giving tool, a gift from our Creator to His creation. God's Word is a sword for battle and a scalpel to separate truth from lies in the most private places of our hearts. It is effective to bind us to our Maker and to make us more like Him.

As we close today, write a prayer below, asking the Lord to teach you to revere His Holy Word. Stand in awe of all it is able to accomplish—in awe of its origin and its Author.

APPROACH TRUTH CONFIDENTLY

Let's take a field trip, shall we?

Today, via your imagination, I'd like to bring you to my house for a little Williams Family game time. Now, brace yourselves: board games around here are an event. They are serious business and insanely silly, all at once. You better come to the table—or floor, or grass, or treehouse—with your game face on because you never know what version of game time you're going to get.

My favorite (slash least favorite) part of game time at our house is what I'll refer to as "The Rule Situation." Sometimes The Rule Situation is pretty straight-forward—we read the rules of the game, we follow the rules of the game. Done and done. Other times, The Rule Situation is a tad more complicated. This is especially true when one of our three children decides to make his or her own rules for the rest of us gamers to follow. Some of you may have experienced this type of kid-rule drama firsthand; but if you haven't, suffice it to say, things can get pretty dicey.

We grown-ups like to think we have a better understanding of how rules work, since we live in the real world and all. Only the official rules count. You can't make up random rules and expect folks to follow. (Well, you can, but your made-up rules don't change what is true. Also, people won't like you and you might get arrested.)

But isn't that how we sometimes approach the Bible? We're given the inspired, complete, and sufficient Word of God, and we are invited to read it by and with the Author Himself. Yet, instead of running to accept the invitation, we trip over our own made-up rules, citing all the reasons we think we don't deserve to go.

Who are we to come to God's Word just as we are? Well, let's take a look inside Scripture and see!

If you are a follower of Jesus—someone who has repented of her sin and trusts Jesus Christ as her Savior—here is a sampling of what God says about *you* in His Word.

1.   I am a child of God (John 1:12).
2.   I am clothed with the righteousness of Jesus (Isaiah 61:10).
3.   I am free (Galatians 5:1).
4.   I am not condemned (Romans 8:1).
5.   I am a new creation (2 Corinthians 5:17).
6.   I am loved (Ephesians 5:2).

In the space below, list some false rules you make up for yourself as qualifications for approaching God's Word. (I've filled in the first two as examples.)

1.   *I must always have the desire to open my Bible.*

2.   *I need to understand everything I read in Scripture.*

3.

4.

5.

6.

I have my own list of false qualifications and I try to hold it up as true alongside the list of truths God Himself speaks about me in His Word. My list includes some admirable qualities, but I too easily forget that my false qualifications, however commendable, are always and forever trumped by God's grace. I can't hold both lists up as true at the same time—it doesn't work.

I'll show you what I mean.

Imagine these lists—God's and yours—side by side with an invisible line connecting the 1s, the 2s, and so on. Now, form a new sentence by combining the two corresponding parts with the phrase "only if" or "because."

What pattern do you see? Does the first list truly depend on the second?

Let's combine my item number 1s as an example:

From His list:
"I am a child of God."

From my list:
"I must always have the desire to open my Bible."

Combined:
*"I am a child of God **only if** I always have the desire to open my Bible."*

Following this pattern, write your new qualification sentences below. Are these new statements true? Do they line up with what God says about your identity in Christ? If not, go ahead and label them as "false"!

My combined statements look something like this:

I am free **because** *I understand everything I read in Scripture.*

I am a new creation **only if** *I have my quiet time at 5 o'clock each morning.*

I am loved **because** *I have read my Bible cover to cover.*

No! These statements are false! When I add my made-up qualifications for Bible-reading to the truths God has spoken over me, I end up with a distorted, false gospel—a gospel of works, not grace. I am not loved *because of* how many pages of the Bible I've read or *because of* how much of it I understand; I am loved because Jesus, in His mercy, loves me. I am not a new creation *if* I wake up at 5:00 each morning (far from it!); I am a new creation because Jesus in His mercy saved me.

The items on God's list are true always and only because of Him. Nothing I do or don't do can change them.

OPEN YOUR BIBLE AND READ HEBREWS 4:14-16.

What adjective does the author of Hebrews use to describe the way we should approach God?

Jesus not only knows our weakness, He understands it. Our High Priest Himself—the One who ushers us to God's throne and into the sacred space of Scripture—experienced temptation and isolation, humiliation and pain, yet did not sin. **Jesus' perfection is both the justification and the mandate for our boldness before God's throne.**

May we, as daughters of the King, approach the Bible with confidence today—not because of who we are, but because of who we are *in Him*.

DAY THREE
APPROACH TRUTH REGULARLY

My sister just had a new baby.

My adorable nephew Leo needs to be fed every 4 hours, and his mama doesn't mind one bit. Food is as crucial as air to his brand-new, tiny, and vulnerable body. When he's been separated from her for more than a few hours, he lets us know with his gummy, squeaky newborn cry. Mama's milk is important, and it's urgent.

OPEN YOUR BIBLE AND READ PSALM 1. (GOODNESS, I LOVE THIS PSALM!)

> **In what does the "blessed" person delight? How often does he meditate on God's law?**

In the very next verse, David describes this righteous person as a tree planted by streams of water. Not a horse who visits the stream from time to time, not a camel who visits the water as needed, but a rooted tree which does not leave its lifesource. The tree and the stream are in relationship with one another.

Like milk to a newborn baby, the stream is important to the tree. But if we could see to the tree's roots, we'd see the relationship is more than important—*it's urgent.* It's non-negotiable. If the tree's connection to water is lost, so is its life.

It's the same with us. We can't approach God's Word only occasionally, expecting our lives not to wither. God designed us to need Him, to be in ongoing relationship with Him as our only lifesource. And like the tree in Psalm 1, we bear fruit in season. The good stuff comes in good time—in God's time.

I want to be that tree. I want *you* to be that tree. I want our roots to be so saturated in the truth of God's Word—not just acknowledging its existence but digging into it, drawing life from it—that our lives bear fruit even on the hardest of days.

So, let's get practical. Many of us, myself included, live in constant tension between "How can I conveniently squeeze Bible-time into my busy schedule?" and "How can my busy schedule reflect the importance of God's Word in my life?" Do you struggle here, too?

Look again at verse 3 of Psalm 1. What is the benefit of being planted by the stream?

Now read verses 4-5. What is at risk if we starve our souls of the nutrients of God's Word?

Proverbs 25:25 says good news from a far country is "like cold water to a thirsty soul" (ESV). Think of a time your soul has "withered" for lack of connection to God and His Word (maybe that time is now).

What does "withered" feel like? How does it feel to reconnect to your lifesource?

What does it take for us to be spiritually healthy and "bear fruit in season"?

Regularly approaching God's Word begins with space and quiet. Sometimes that's found in the sweet and sacred morning hours before the rest of the world wakes. Sometimes it's when you arrive early in the school pick-up line or during a lunch hour at work. In situations that may look more convenient than purposeful, there is still relationship—and God promises a life rooted in Him will bear fruit!

Even in the dry season, may our souls remain steeped in the unending goodness and love of our Savior as found in His Word.

PRAY

Read through Psalm 1 again, and choose a section to write as a prayer in the space below.

APPROACH TRUTH PRAYERFULLY

My mother-in-law makes the best salsa.

Not only is it made with all fresh ingredients and the right combination of seasoning and Groovy love (yes, my kids call their grandmother "Groovy"), but her vegetables always look perfectly diced and evenly distributed. Every attempt I made at her salsa recipe was less impressive with twice the effort, so I just assumed Groovy was part wizard.

The summer after Ryan and I were married, we visited his parents' home in Michigan. Ryan requested his mom's chips and salsa as soon as we walked in the door and she happily obliged. Then, to my complete surprise and delight, she reached into her kitchen cabinet and produced a Vidalia Chop Wizard™, which I have since renamed "The Best Kitchen Tool Ever" (BKTE, for short). My mind was simultaneously blown and thrilled as I discovered that I, too, could have perfectly chopped salsa—just like my mother-in-law!

It's been twelve years since that glorious day, and I've been singing that chopper's praises ever since—quite effectively, too, I might add. If only Groovy had bought stock in this "as seen on TV" wonder, she'd be a wealthy woman!

Don't you just love it when you find a fantastic tool that finally accomplishes what you've never been able to achieve on your own? Like the "topsy tail" in the 90s and the green stopper-stick that keeps your hot coffee from spilling—to one degree or another, these tools are game changers.

Prayer, like the BKTE, is a powerful tool. It has the power to do things we cannot do on our own.

Prayer isn't just a game changer—it's a heart changer. It not only affords us direct access to the Author of the Universe, it allows us to confess and repent, intercede and petition, and offer thanks and praise wherever and whenever we choose.

But as wonderful and effective as prayer is, it's more than a privilege; it's an imperative.

OPEN YOUR BIBLE TO THE VERSES BELOW. WHAT IS THE APOSTLE PAUL'S IMPERATIVE TO THE CHURCHES OF PHILIPPI AND THESSALONICA?

PHILIPPIANS 4:6

In _____, through prayer and petition with thanksgiving, let your requests be made known to God.

1 THESSALONIANS 5:17

Pray _____.

Because prayer is the powerful tool and imperative act of every Christian, **effective Bible reading can and should begin and end with prayer.** As we studied in Week One, every word of Scripture is inspired by the Holy Spirit (2 Tim. 3:16; 2 Pet. 1:21). We also know the Spirit was sent to be our Helper (John 14:16). So, why would we ever pass up the opportunity to invite the Author to join us as we approach the text? It's a director's commentary at the ready!

You know one great way to do that? With Scripture!

OPEN YOUR BIBLE AND WRITE DAVID'S PRAYER FROM PSALM 119:18 BELOW. THIS IS AN EXCELLENT PRAYER OF INVITATION AS WE OPEN OUR BIBLES!

PSALM 119:18

Prayer is also an appropriate and intentional way to conclude our time in God's Word. Isaiah 40:8 is one of my favorite verses to pray as I close my Bible.

OPEN YOUR BIBLE AND WRITE THE WORDS FROM ISAIAH 40:8 BELOW:

ISAIAH 40:8

Below are a few more passages which serve as excellent, prayerful starting points as we approach God's Word. Take some time now to read each passage and write a short prayer using its words. This collection of prayers will be a resource you can refer back to as you open and close your Bible in the days and years to come.

Note: As you work down this list, consider writing some of these verses/prayers on notecards to put in your Bible or at a place where you often sit to read your Bible and pray. Let them serve as a reminder and guide as you approach God's Word!

SCRIPTURE TO PRAY AS YOU OPEN YOUR BIBLE:

Here's an example:

JOHN 16:13-15, ESV

> **PASSAGE:** *When the Spirit of truth comes, he will guide you into all the truth, for he will not speak on his own authority, but whatever he hears he will speak, and he will declare to you the things that are to come. He will glorify me, for he will take what is mine and declare it to you. All that the Father has is mine; therefore I said that he will take what is mine and declare it to you.*

> **PRAYER:** *Spirit of truth, come and guide me in all the truth. Take what is the Father's and declare it to me!*

EZEKIEL 36:27

> **PASSAGE:** *I will place My Spirit within you and cause you to follow My statutes and carefully observe My ordinances.*

> **PRAYER:**

PSALM 25:5

> **PASSAGE:** *Guide me in Your truth and teach me, for You are the God of my salvation; I wait for You all day long.*

PRAYER:

PSALM 119:27, ESV

> **PASSAGE:** *Make me understand the way of your precepts, and I will meditate on your wondrous works.*

PRAYER:

JOHN 14:26

> **PASSAGE:** *But the Counselor, the Holy Spirit—the Father will send Him in My name—will teach you all things and remind you of everything I have told you.*

PRAYER:

SCRIPTURE TO PRAY AS YOU CLOSE YOUR BIBLE:

Here's an example:

2 SAMUEL 7:28, ESV

> **PASSAGE:** *And now, O Lord God, you are God, and your words are true, and you have promised this good thing to your servant.*
>
> **PRAYER:** *O Lord God, you are God and your words are true.*

PSALM 119:103

> **PASSAGE:** *How sweet Your word is to my taste—sweeter than honey in my mouth.*
>
> **PRAYER:**

2 TIMOTHY 3:16-17

> **PASSAGE:** *All Scripture is inspired by God and is profitable for teaching, for rebuking, for correcting, for training in righteousness, so that the man of God may be complete, equipped for every good work.*
>
> **PRAYER:**

WEEK 3

ENGAGE TRUTH

I kill plants.

It's a thing I do. I'm not particularly proud of it, but I no longer feel the need to deny it either. A green thumb is just not part of my makeup. I keep thinking one day I'll grow into it (pardon the pun), but so far, not so good.

One thing I've learned in my years of plant killing is that they need water to survive (Botanists, take note!). The concept is simple enough: water the plant and it lives. Fail to water the plant and it withers and dies. My problem is, I only think about watering my flower beds when I'm driving the kids to school. I remember the houseplant is dying when I'm sitting at the conference room table. It's not that I want to kill the plants. It's just that I don't make caring for them a priority, so they suffer.

As much as I wish I could, I can't water plants with my good intentions. They need actual water, honest-to-goodness H_2O, to live. I have to follow my intention with action.

When the Samaritan woman encountered Jesus at the well, He said if she *only knew* who was standing before her, she would ask Him for living water. She would ask for the water that would quench her thirst not just that day but forevermore.

I *do* know who Jesus is. Chances are you do too, or you wouldn't be reading this. Yet, like the woman at the well, I dip my bucket into water that cannot satisfy. As if my heart and soul are as inconsequential as a houseplant, I've gone days and weeks without filling up on the Living Water and living Word. **I nourish my life with good intentions and expect it to thrive when only Jesus can quench my soul-deep thirst.**

Friends, if we want to engage this Book the way it is intended—with our heart, soul, mind, and strength—and glean from it the fullness of the life it gives, we must come to it daily, expecting to be filled. We won't always want to read the Bible. There will be days when we are angry, hurt, tired, or spent. But the Word of God is for us even then—especially then!

We engage God's Word to see the beauty of Jesus and the gospel of redemption. We come time and time again, and He promises to water us well. The Living Water satisfies our thirst for truth, love, and grace like no one and nothing else can.

LOOKING BACK:

Last week we examined our preconceived notions about what qualifies us to approach God's Word. Looking back at "Your List" in Day Two, share one of the false qualifications you struggle with. Is there a passage of Scripture we've read this week that can help you combat that lie with truth?

Baby Leo and the Psalm 1 tree reminded us that opening our Bibles is not only important, it's urgent. Talk about the things in your daily life that are urgent. What do you think causes us to place so many of those things above spending time with God in His Word? What would happen if we didn't? Would those other urgent things benefit or suffer?

In Day Four, you formed prayers from Scripture to pray as you open and close your Bible. Is praying Scripture a new experience for you? Choose one of those "Open Your Bible" prayers to pray now with your group as you move into today's study.

WATCH THE VIDEO:

To hear more from Raechel and Amanda, download the optional video bundle to view Week Three at *www.lifeway.com/openyourbible.*

NOW, LET'S TALK:

OPEN YOUR BIBLE TO JOHN 4:7-15 AND READ IT TOGETHER.

> What is the woman's response when Jesus tells her the effect the living water will have on her life?

> Notice how quickly she responds to Jesus' invitation. How would you respond?

OPEN YOUR BIBLE AGAIN, AND LET'S READ THE VERSES BEFORE AND AFTER THE PASSAGE ABOVE, OVERLAPPING JUST A LITTLE.

READ JOHN 4:1-8.

> What do you notice now that you're engaging the passage more broadly? Whose well was this? Why is that significant?

> How does the fact that this story happened in a real time and place change the way you view Scripture? How does it change the way you receive Jesus' words as truth?

NOW READ VERSES 15-26.

> What are the empty wells the Samaritan woman drew from in her own life? Did Jesus disqualify her from His invitation because she was broken, or did He offer the water because she was empty?

> What are some empty wells you go to each day in search of life-giving water? How are those different than the water Jesus describes in verse 14?

> Like we read in Amanda's plant-killing story in the "Start Here," what would it be like to stop nourishing our lives with good intentions and empty wells? If we water our lives by daily engaging the Living Word, how would we flourish in ways we are wilting today?

Don't let your emptiness keep you from coming to the well. Come to the well to be filled.

A well-marked
Bible is the sign of
a well-fed soul.
Charles Spurgeon

DAY ONE
ENGAGE TRUTH EXPECTANTLY

I've had a Bible for as long as I can remember.

Last year our family moved, and I unpacked several Bibles of various translations onto our favorite bookshelf, the one in the foyer made of weathered doors and old windows. My children have Bibles of their own. My daughter has a tiny, pale pink New Testament her grandparents gave her when she was a baby, and now she has a "big girl" Bible given to her on her seventh birthday. My twin boys each have a Bible with a sword on the cover, presented at their baptism, and a comic book Bible to share (because they are superheroes, of course).

> The Bible is part of my life and always has been. (I mean, it was my last name for the first 25 years of my life. What's a girl to do?) But for the longest time I ignored the bulk of Scripture for one simple reason—I only wanted to know Jesus.
>
> I wanted to know the Jesus who looked at a woman caught in sin—a woman others were prepared to stone, the rocks already in their hands—and said to her, "Neither do I condemn you; go ... sin no more" (John 8:11, ESV).
>
> I wanted to know the Jesus who made breakfast for His disciples on the beach while they cast their nets to the place He instructed and hauled in 153 fish (John 21:11).
>
> I wanted to know the Jesus who, while dying a criminal's death on the cross for my sin, taught me it's never too soon to forgive (Luke 23:34) and never too late to be forgiven (Luke 23:43).
>
> I wanted to know Him—*really* know Him. And so I stuck to the books of the Bible I thought were about Him.

What parts of the Bible have you frequented in the past? Do you tend to visit the same familiar books, or do you often venture into new-to-you territory? Why do you think that is?

After a few decades of living with the Bible, I finally learned a glorious truth: all of Scripture points to Jesus. Every book, every page, every sentence points to the goodness of our God and the truth of His Son. The beauty and perfection of His heart, the relentless pursuit of His people, and His plan to rescue the souls of men and women from the vice grip of sin and darkness—this is the plot line of every book of the Bible.

It's all about Jesus.

OPEN YOUR BIBLE AND READ JOHN 5:39-40.

Who is speaking here? Whom is He speaking to? Look at verses 16-18 for context.

Read verse 39 again. What did the Jewish leaders expect to find when searching the Scriptures?

Can you think of a time when you opened your Bible to find religion instead of Jesus? What caused you to approach Scripture that way? What was the result?

Time and time again, Jesus rebuked the Jewish leaders for placing their faith in religion rather than God. When I think of the ways I've used the Bible as a religious prop in my own life, I wonder if I would have found myself standing alongside the Pharisees. *Am I merely seeking the trappings and gold stars of the Bible-toting Christian life, or am I seeking Christ Himself?*

After His resurrection from the dead, Jesus gathered with His disciples and ate in front of them, encouraging them to touch His hands and feet and *believe*. Then He revealed to them a crucial truth about the centerpiece of the Story.

OPEN YOUR BIBLE AND READ LUKE 24:25-27 AND 44-48.

Jesus tells His disciples that the Law, the Prophets, and the Psalms are written about whom? Look again at verse 47—what does Jesus point to as the primary message of the Scriptures?

Because each page of Scripture points to Jesus, we can open our Bibles and expect to find Him there—today and tomorrow, in the Old Testament or the New, grownups and superheroes alike.

The Bible is for you and for now, but it is about God. It has been all along.

ENGAGE TRUTH EMOTIONALLY AND INTELLECTUALLY

I'm an emoter.

If the first half of my Christian life were made into a film, it would most certainly be a Hallmark movie—heavy on feeling, light on substance. (Apologies to any Hallmark movie producers in the house. We all [secretly] love you.)

I'm a girl who's always prized the academic perspective of things—my other dream job is Professional Student—but when it came to my relationship with Jesus, I thought the point was to *feel* something. If I didn't have an emotional experience, then I must not have experienced God. This was the unspoken premise I operated under.

How do you naturally engage Scripture—emotionally or intellectually?

Have you relied too heavily on one approach or the other? If so, what might you be missing?

It wasn't until college that I truly began to engage the Bible with my intellectual self. It all started when I heard that "grace" word thrown around as if it had something to do with faith. Those five letters flipped my good Christian world on its head, and I dug into every book I could find about grace and the gospel of Jesus. A good thing to do, right? And it was. I learned so much about God and myself in my time of grace-digging. It was as if I'd uncovered the hidden nugget I'd been out hunting for with my metal detector all along.

The problem—and because we're sinners, there is always a problem—was that I overcorrected. I went from Amanda Feels-A-Lot to Amanda Studies-A-Lot overnight, the pendulum swinging so far and so quickly it gave me spiritual whiplash. I wasn't sure what to believe or how to believe it.

So, which is it? Are we to engage God's Word emotionally, intellectually, or both?

OPEN YOUR BIBLE TO JOHN 4. EARLIER THIS WEEK WE READ ABOUT JESUS' ENCOUNTER WITH THE SAMARITAN WOMAN AT THE WELL. TODAY LET'S READ VERSES 16-26 AGAIN.

What information is the Samaritan woman trying to get from Jesus in verse 20?

According to Jesus' words in verse 23, what kind of worshiper does God seek?

READ VERSE 24 AND FILL IN THE BLANKS:

God is _____, and those who worship Him must worship

in _____ and _____.

The Samaritan woman was asking about the *where* of worship, but Jesus was more concerned with the *how*. To worship the Father in spirit and in truth, we must engage His Word both emotionally *and* intellectually. **We must come to God with our whole self.**

OPEN YOUR BIBLE AND READ MATTHEW 22:37-38.

In what three ways are we to love the Lord? What do you think is significant about the fact that Jesus lists all three together?

ENGAGE TRUTH EMOTIONALLY

The Psalms are an excellent and approachable example of what it looks like to come to God with our whole selves. Rather than check their emotions at the door, the psalmists engage in prayer and worship with their emotional self fully intact.

OPEN YOUR BIBLE AND READ PSALM 13.

How was the psalmist feeling at the time he penned this particular psalm?

Turn to the first verse of Psalm 10. What emotions do you hear in those opening questions?

Reading the Psalms reminds me that God does not despise my humanity but welcomes me, by the grace of Christ, to His Word and His throne just as I am. Engaging truth emotionally is not only allowed, it is appropriate!

At the same time, we know that God's thoughts are not our thoughts. Isaiah 55:8-9 tells us they are infinitely higher. How then do we engage our intellect in such an undertaking?

ENGAGE TRUTH INTELLECTUALLY

OPEN YOUR BIBLE TO ROMANS 12:1-2.

According to verse 2, is our mind a part of our spiritual transformation in Christ? How do you know?

What is the product of a transformed mind?

Observing cultural and historical context is a wonderful example of how engaging truth intellectually can inform our understanding and experience of Scripture. Take the Mountains of Moriah, for example. Here Abraham offered up Isaac as a sacrifice in Genesis 22:2. Centuries later, as recorded in 2 Chronicles 3:1, Solomon built his temple on these same mountains. Mount Moriah may also be the place of Golgotha, the hill on which Christ was crucified. Fascinating, right?

Knowing historical context doesn't just serve as fodder for good dinner conversation—it also helps to keep us rooted in the reality of the gospel and the veracity of Scripture.

Engaging truth in only one way, whether with the most delicate emotions or the most advanced intellect, is to forfeit a full and true understanding of it. **The gospel is a beautiful marriage of mind and spirit, and God's Word is meant to be engaged by our intellect and emotions.**

We'll each sway back and forth, tending to one or the other, and that's okay. God can handle our swaying. What He asks is that we bring Him all of us, every time—love for cheesy movies and all.

ENGAGE TRUTH BROADLY

We called it my "Meat Party."

For my birthday last year, my husband hosted a dinner party at our house, complete with white linens, fancy drinks, a few obligatory greens, and eight enormous, juicy, salty steaks off the grill.

You see, my favorite food is steak. Or, to be slightly more general, I love any hot, salty meat, really. My friends laugh and cringe a little when I say it, but anyone who knows me knows this passion of mine.

I'm sure I lost a handful of you at "hot, salty meat," but it's the truth. For me, meat can be the appetizer, entree, and dessert. Basically the entire meal.

Now, the Bible was never actually referred to as our Daily Steak (which is unfortunate), but if it had been, I'd absolutely relate. I am also certain it was never called our Daily Snack. *Daily Bread implies survival.* It is necessary. It is sustenance.

You know when the deer *pants* for the water in Psalm 42? The psalmist says *that's* how he feels about God. He's not a little thirsty—he's parched and panting for the Lord.

I have to pause here for a moment to ask:

When was the last time you were desperate and panting—in need of God?

When was the last time you craved His Word like your favorite meal?

OPEN YOUR BIBLE TO 1 SAMUEL 1:12-16.

Hannah prayed desperately to the Lord in the temple, so desperately that Eli accused her of what?

OPEN YOUR BIBLE TO JOB 23:12.

Job's hunger for the infinite was greater than his hunger for the finite. What does he say about the words of God's mouth?

OPEN YOUR BIBLE TO THE FOLLOWING VERSES.

Copy them down, and pray the words as you write, asking God to increase your hunger for and satisfaction in His Word.

PSALM 119:97

PSALM 119:127

PSALM 119:131

I've been convicted lately to read my Bible more broadly than just a few verses or even a chapter a day—to consume it as a hearty meal, rather than an hors d'oeuvre. And as I have begun to change the way I engage God's Word, I can't help but wonder: *If I read my Bible as often as I read other books (or blogs, texts, and social media), would I manage to read it from cover to cover in only a month or two?*

The truth is, we can (and should) tackle whole books at once, reading shorter ones straight through and repeatedly, every day for a week or a month, to really engage it fully. It's not the only way or "right way" to read the Bible, but it's a powerful exercise in engaging God's Word as a complete work, and an effective way to deepen our understanding of His story.

Reading things other than the Bible is absolutely okay. But reflect for a moment and list some things you may be guzzling more eagerly than God's Word.

Think of the last time you sat down to the Bible for a long read. What was it like? Did it make you even hungrier for God's Word?

What if we were women who craved and consumed God's Word for the meal it is intended to be? What if we "read on" when the rest of the world moved on? If we kept on drinking the Living Water, what would we find at the bottom of our glasses? Would we ever reach the bottom?

By approaching Scripture broadly, we have so much to learn! We probably shouldn't call it a "meat party," but we can be absolutely certain that guzzling Scripture will take us from parched to quenched like nothing this fading world can ever offer. (But if you ever do throw a Bible Meat Party, please count me in!)

LET'S TRY APPROACHING THE BIBLE AS A MEAL TODAY. HERE ARE A FEW SUGGESTIONS:

- *Curl up with God's Word and consume five chapters straight—even an entire book!*
- *Try the Book of 3 John—it's only 219 words. The Book of Colossians would be an awesome choice, too!*
- *Read the rest of 1 Samuel 1 to find out what happened when Hannah faithfully prayed to the Lord in her desperation.*
- *Read Matthew 14 all the way through to understand what news was fresh in Jesus' heart just before He preached to and fed the five thousand.*
- *Read 2 Samuel 11 & 12 to get the full story of Bathsheba. We think of her as the rooftop bather and the source of David's lust, but do you know whose mother she is?*

ENGAGE TRUTH PRAYERFULLY

I'm always late. Always.

I know—it's incredibly annoying. Trust me, I'm annoyed, too. But this is one of the things you need to know about me if we're going to be friends. At this point I've determined the condition is due to some type of personality disorder for which there is no cure.

> You also need to know about the piles. There are certain dark corners of our house where we stash, you know, *stuff*. Stacks of papers to be sorted, piles of various things to be put away, boxes of CDs we don't know what to do with because we can't bear to fully embrace the digital music age (raise your hand if you're still mourning the death of the mixtape).
>
> The hallway of our new-old home doesn't have a light in it, so it's dark and a little gloomy most hours of the day. This drove me crazy until I realized it helped disguise the piles of folded laundry in the corner. And the dust bunnies on the hardwood floor (I'm also not the best housekeeper, you guys).
>
> **There's a kind of unsettled comfort in keeping the messy parts of our lives out of the light. There is comfort, but not peace.**
>
> When you and I open our Bibles and engage God's Word, we are also encountering the Living Word, Jesus Christ. *We are encountering Light Himself.*

OPEN YOUR BIBLE TO JOHN 1:1-5 AND READ CLOSELY THE OPENING LINES FROM JOHN'S GOSPEL. GO BACK THROUGH THE PASSAGE A SECOND TIME, CIRCLING EACH USE OF THE WORD "WORD" AND UNDERLINING THE WORDS "LIFE" AND "LIGHT."

JOHN 1:1-5

> *In the beginning was the Word,*
> *and the Word was with God,*
> *and the Word was God.*
> *He was with God in the beginning.*
> *All things were created through Him,*
> *and apart from Him not one thing was created*
> *that has been created.*
> *Life was in Him,*
> *and that life was the light of men.*
> *That light shines in the darkness,*
> *yet the darkness did not overcome it.*

When we immerse ourselves in the pure, undimmable truth of God's Word, its brightness will inevitably reveal our heart's darkest corners. Like those unlit corners of my messy house, it won't be pretty. But this conviction of sin—of the heart's tendency to darkness—is another important role of the Holy Spirit.

When we invite the Holy Spirit through prayer to be our guide and companion, we are also inviting Him to drag us into the light of Jesus. It is there that we can confess our sin, repent of its filth, receive unreserved forgiveness, and be reconciled to God.

OPEN YOUR BIBLE AND READ PROVERBS 3:3-12.

Verses 5-6 may be familiar to you. How is your understanding of those verses enriched when read in the context of the broader passage?

What can we learn from verses 11-12 about the gift of conviction by the Holy Spirit?

Most of my life I assumed becoming a "good Christian" was the goal: doing, or appearing to do, all the right things, and keeping sin at bay or at least out of the light. I mistook the narrow road of Matthew 7:14 as the path of least spiritual resistance.

Yet, as we travel through the pages of Scripture and grow in the knowledge of God, we find our need for the gospel does not magically become smaller. Instead, we more clearly see the enormity of our need. Our salvation is an order so tall only Christ's perfection can measure up, a gap so large only His mercy can fill.

What about you? What do you perceive as the goal of a "good Christian"?

What does verse 8 say about those who believe they are without sin?

Copy verse 9 below.

The Light is necessary for us to see our sin. What is God's promise to those who confess their sin to Him?

Opening our Bibles every day is not all rainbows and roses—it is hard work. It requires discipline and obedience, and it brings us face to face with the ugly reality of our sin. It brings us to our knees in repentance, asking once again for the light of Christ to overcome our darkness. *And He does.*

Somewhere in the thick of this ongoing heart surgery we begin to understand: **only in seeing the depth of our sin can we know the unmatched grace and glory of the cross.**

Friends, let's ask the Holy Spirit for the gift of conviction today. And let's pray, ten times over, that we may see with unhindered eyes the cross of Jesus that covers our sin.

PSST.

LEAN IN. WE HAVE A SECRET TO SHARE WITH YOU.

Now that you're officially halfway through this study (Yay! Way to go, you!), you're probably well aware of the heartbeat for this little book: *The Bible is for you and for now.*

Whether you're learning this beautiful truth for the first time or being reminded of it anew, we pray it is taking root in your heart, seeping deep into your bones, and coloring the world around you. God's Word is living and active, you guys! This is good, good news.

What you don't yet know is that we have another huge, audacious prayer for this book—a secret hope we've been excitedly waiting to share with you!

Go to *www.lifeway.com/openyourbible* and watch (for free!) the **Open Your Bible Invitation.**

Our prayer is this: *as you discover that the Bible is for you and for now, we pray you'll invite other women into this same life-changing truth.*

Have any of those walls standing between you and God's Word begun to crumble? Is the Lord is setting you free from false expectations or guilt as we confess our fears and explore His truth together? Is the Holy Spirit exposing misconceptions about truth in your head and heart as we read what Scripture says about Scripture?

If the answer to any of these questions is *yes*, imagine other women experiencing that same freedom!

The friend you run into at school drop-off ...

The coworker you grab lunch with ...

The women in your Sunday school class ...

The neighbor you chat with over the fence ...

The sister you know is lonely and hurting ...

WHAT WOULD IT BE LIKE TO INVITE OTHERS ALONG ON THIS JOURNEY OF OPENING OUR BIBLES?

Some of you already feel your chest tightening at the thought. Others are reaching to turn the page. This suggestion might make you uncomfortable—but that's okay! You know why? *Because inviting women to open their Bibles does not have to be a perfectly planned, elegantly executed event.* It doesn't have to be an event at all!

It can be you and a friend over morning coffee.

It can be a group of your besties sitting in a circle on the floor of your living room.

It can be Monday night Skype™ sessions with your roommates from college or a weekly FaceTime with your niece.

It can be whatever you and the Lord dream up! (And He's creative enough to come up with something great, don't you think?)

RIGHT NOW, TODAY, WE ONLY HAVE ONE BIG ASK: PRAY.

Ask God to soften your heart on behalf of the other women in your life, that you would long for them to know that the Bible is for *them* and for *now*.

Ask Him to plant in your heart the seeds of what it could look like for you to invite other women to open their Bibles alongside you.

If you'd like a friend to join you in leading other women in this study, ask God to provide that person! (Jesus often sent disciples out in twos. Could your Bible-opening buddy be in your group today?)

Above all, pray for the Holy Spirit to continue His work in you (just like He promises He will in Philippians 1:6), teaching you that God's Word is for you, for now, and about Him.

We're praying with you!

Praise be to God for the good gift of His Word. Amen.

xo,

APPLY TRUTH

*I've been having ill thoughts
toward my mirror lately.*

I'm feeling a bit betrayed by the looking glass, annoyed that it doesn't return a leaner, smoother, more toned and together version of me. It isn't that I lack truth to combat the tornado of lies swirling in my head; I know I should love myself as I am, be thankful for my health, remember that I'm a cherished daughter made in the image of a loving and beautiful God. And I do! I am! I try. But it's tough to keep those truths in my head connected to my heart.

When it comes to taking care of my body and having a truth-filled perception of it, I find myself wishing for magic beans like the ones that grew Jack's beanstalk high into the clouds. I don't necessarily need the easiest way out, but a quick one would be nice. Maybe a tried and true one-time workout that turns my metabolism back a couple decades? Or a two-day meal plan that gives me the energy of a caffeinated toddler? I'd prefer the results without the process, or at least a game plan I know will work because I can *see* it working.

I fight this same internal battle when it comes to applying God's Word to my life. The concept is confusing to me. *What does application mean exactly? Does God's Word itself change me, or is my feeble attempt at applying it to my life the "on" switch that activates the process? How does it work and how do I know it's working?*

Not unlike my struggle with my physical self, I find myself wishing for a fast track to bypass all the hard work and question marks, a spiritual version of those convenient, Nobel prize-worthy moving floors in the airport—the ones that whisk me the entire length of a terminal with just a few casual steps. Why can't applying Scripture be like *that*?

My pastor's wife and I were chatting recently about this mystery of cause and effect. Suddenly, she stopped me mid-sentence and with wild eyes declared, "Skincare!" I knew it immediately: the woman is a genius.

I bought my first "real" skincare products well into my thirties. That is, about 15 years too late.

That smooth countenance I wish for when I look in the mirror? It requires actually taking steps to care for my skin. This means more than swallowing my pride and asking the woman at the cosmetic counter to instruct me on proper face-washing (bless my heart), and it means more than buying the products she recommends. It requires me actually using that knowledge and those products—not just once, but daily. Even the fancy face creams the celebrities use do nothing if left in the pretty jar with the shiny lid. *The face cream may be transformative in nature, but it only works if I apply it.*

If Scripture application is a tricky subject for you, you are not alone! We regularly find ourselves staring at our Bibles like a jar of fancy face cream, wondering, *What happens now, exactly? What part of applying God's Word is up to me? What is the relationship between what I "do" and what the Holy Spirit sovereignly does?*

These are important questions, ones we'll start working through today and continue to explore throughout the week. Let's start with what we do know because God's Word tells us so:

2 PETER 1:3

His divine power has given us everything required for life and godliness through the knowledge of Him who called us by His own glory and goodness.

Those boutique skincare products cost a small fortune, but look! God has given us everything we need for "life and godliness" in His Word, free of charge.

PHILIPPIANS 2:12-13

...work out your own salvation with fear and trembling. For it is God who is working in you, enabling you both to desire and to work out His good purpose.

God is working in us, but there is work for us to do, too. And He has already equipped us, via His Word and Spirit, with all we need to live lives of godliness in the knowledge of Him.

Application does not look like checkmarks on a page. It does not look like an eraser removing my flaws or magic beans that send my spiritual maturity high into the sky. It looks like the Messiah coming close, cupping my face in His hands, and saying: *You are mine. Take my Word into your heart and life today, dear one. Show up. Be still. Listen and believe. Work out your faith, stumble forward in grace. I will do the rest.*

Friends, Scripture is not only meant to be read, it is meant to be applied to our hearts and lives. **God's Word is transformative in its very nature, and it will transform us.**

LOOKING BACK:

Last week we were reminded that all of Scripture points to Jesus—His gospel is the theme of every story! How does it change the rest of your day when you spend time engaging God's Word and find Jesus there? What happens when you start seeing your life as part of His redemptive work in the world?

We are called to engage truth emotionally and intellectually, but most of us tend toward one or the other. Which one are you? Share with your group the blessings and challenges of your point of view. Learn from each other!

How did you react to the concept of engaging truth broadly? Have you ever consumed Scripture by the book or read a large chunk in one sitting? How was that experience different from reading a bite-sized portion?

If you haven't tried reading the Bible broadly, would you like to? Brainstorm some options together!

WATCH THE VIDEO:

To hear more from Raechel and Amanda, download the optional video to view Week Four at *www.lifeway.com/openyourbible.*

NOW, LET'S TALK:

Let's explore the relationship between what God does and what we do. It's a tough conversation, but that's exactly why it is so beautiful to discuss this in the context of our community with each other!

> *APPLICATION IS NOT AN EVENT, IT IS A PROCESS.* *The trappings of a spiritual life mean nothing without the substance, just as having the right products in our medicine cabinet does not give us healthy skin.*

OPEN YOUR BIBLE AND READ PHILIPPIANS 2:1-13.

> **How does your understanding of verses 12-13 change when you read them in light of the 11 verses that come before?**
>
> **Paul instructs us to work out our salvation "with fear and trembling." Why do you think he chose those words?**

> *APPLICATION IS NOT CHECKMARKS ON A PAGE, IT IS A RELATIONSHIP.* *It is an ongoing and active relationship between us and the God who made us, pursues us, and saves us. This is the same God and Savior we just read about in the Philippians passage—our doing is in response to what He has already done.*

OPEN YOUR BIBLE AND READ 2 PETER 1:3-8.

> **According to verse 3, what do you need for life and godliness that you are currently lacking?**
>
> **Still in verse 3, by what means has God given us all we need? Do you feel the freedom in that promise? (We do! Our praise hands are in the air over here!)**
>
> **Now look at verse 5. Knowing you've been given all you need, how does that change the way you receive Peter's instructions to "make every effort to supplement your faith" with that long list of good things? Does it give you confidence?**
>
> **Do you feel more or less compelled to work out your faith knowing Christ is already at work in you? Explain.**

APPLICATION IS NOT PROBLEM-SOLVING, IT IS FAITHFULNESS. It is reading the truth and rubbing it in, day after day. It is believing the gospel daily and walking in grace.

OPEN YOUR BIBLE *TO EPHESIANS 2:4-10.*

What was our condition when God saved us?

Verse 8 affirms that our redemption is ultimately an act of God, not us. According to verse 10, what is our job as believers? Who prepared our "good works" and when?

PRAY EPHESIANS 2:8 TOGETHER AS A GROUP, THANKING GOD FOR THE SALVATION HE ACCOMPLISHED ON YOUR BEHALF:

Father, thank You for the glorious truth of the gospel—

that we are saved by grace through faith.

This is not from ourselves. It is Your gift to us!

We remember and rejoice in that gift together today.

Amen.

God's Word is transformative and it will transform us.

For every
look at yourself,
take ten looks at Christ.
He is altogether lovely.

ROBERT MURRAY
M'CHEYNE

DAY ONE

APPLY TRUTH APPROPRIATELY

I used to think reading my Bible was about me.

When I was in junior high, I flung open my turquoise Student Study Bible any time I needed a pick-me-up or some friend advice. I wanted God's Word to work like a vending machine—just punch in the right letters and numbers, and out pops a little something to satisfy my latest craving. To me, the Bible was full of moral lessons that were immediately useful and directly applicable to my current situation. Context or no context, I wanted everything in the Bible to be either *about* me or a direct word *to* me.

Maybe this is why I arrived at adulthood involuntarily cringing anytime the word "apply" was used in reference to the Bible. I have grown weary of extrapolating a pithy moral every time I open my Bible, like cracking open a fortune cookie after enjoying a plate of Kung Pao chicken. As I have grown in my relationship with God, I've learned that a tidy takeaway isn't what I'm really after anyway.

What words do you think of when you hear the term "apply"?

What positive and negative emotions does the word bring up for you?

The Bible indeed contains all we need to know for godly living, but we would be foolish to approach God's Word looking only for how it applies to us or others, forgetting to find what it says about Him.

It took years of spiritual growth for me to understand a truth distilled beautifully into these instructions we've heard time and time again: When we open our Bibles, we shouldn't ask, *"What does this mean to me?"* Instead, we should ask, *"What does this mean?"*

Take a look at the passages below, asking each time, "What does this mean?" and "What does this say about God?"

EXODUS 20:2

MALACHI 4:1-3

ROMANS 8:1-4

LUKE 3:21-22

Another common mistake many people make, often unintentionally, is to take well-known verses or phrases and apply them to people or situations out of context. Gordon Fee says in his book *How to Read the Bible for All Its Worth*, "If you take things out of context enough, you can make almost any part of Scripture say anything you want it to. But at that moment you are no longer reading the Bible, you are abusing it."[1]

Below are a few verses commonly misquoted or misunderstood. Look them up and read them in context (with the verses before and after). For a better, more accurate understanding of what the text is saying, ask again, "What does this mean?" instead of "What does this mean for me?"

EXODUS 14:14

PSALM 37:4

ROMANS 8:28

PHILIPPIANS 4:13

Can you think of others to add to this list?

I admit some days I still open my Bible seeking to find myself instead of Jesus. I want His Holy Word to serve me rather than rule me. **It takes God's grace to remember that applying His Word to our hearts is a work of the Holy Spirit, and that it must be applied appropriately.**

LET'S ASK HIM FOR THAT GRACE NOW BY PRAYING THE PRAYER BELOW:

Father, forgive me for the times I've sought You in pursuit of a "good day,"
when what You have to offer me is a good life.
Forgive me for the times I've sought to serve myself
in the Book that teaches me to serve You.
By your Holy Spirit, grant me the grace and discernment
to apply Scripture appropriately.
Amen.

HOW CAN WE AVOID PULLING SCRIPTURE OUT OF CONTEXT?

- Read the full chapter or full section of verses surrounding it.
- Ask: Who is speaking? To whom? What is happening?
- Read the passage in various Bible translations.
- Consult a Bible commentary to learn more about the setting, situation, and cultural clues.

A great example: In some translations (like ESV), God tells Israel in Amos 4:6, "I gave you cleanness of teeth," which we might take to mean the Lord is blessing Israel with oral health. Other translations clarify that "clean teeth" is a cultural way of saying "I gave you empty stomachs" (NIV) or, "I gave you absolutely nothing to eat" (HCSB). What a difference a little context makes!

APPLY TRUTH RESPONSIBLY

First do no harm.

It's the vow a physician upholds when using a scalpel. Shouldn't it also be ours when wielding the holy and powerful Word of God?

Back in Week Two, we talked about approaching the Bible with reverence, finding it compared to a double-edged sword and even named the Sword of the Spirit. But we'd be kidding ourselves to ignore the truth that this weapon can be wielded not just in an honorable way for God's glory, but in a dishonorable way for our own. Misconstruing or misusing God's Word can cause real hurt to others, and those honest-to-goodness cuts don't heal quickly or easily.

We could leave the conversation here, moving on under the assumption we'll all do our best to handle the Sword of the Spirit and each other with care. But if you're willing, I'd like to wade into these waters a little further.

How does reverence extend to our application of Scripture? How do we responsibly apply God's Word, both within ourselves and in our relationships with others?

Let's pause here and ask ourselves some tough but necessary questions. When have you been hurt by people misusing God's Word?

What specific Scripture verses or passages have you seen used to justify hurting others?

If we were having this particular conversation in person (I wish we were!), I'd ask if you know anyone who has been hurt in this way, and I bet you'd say yes. If we could look each other in the eye, I might even be able to tell from your countenance if that person is you. Then I'd tell you that I've been that person, too—sometimes from a misuse of my own making.

Have you ever misused Scripture to injure yourself? Have you ever taken God's truth and fashioned it into a false gospel or used it as a means to justify excess guilt or overt legalism? Confess those to the Lord now using the space below.

Many of you reading these words have personal and tender stories on the topic of spiritual or scriptural abuse. Before we read on, hear these promises from Scripture today. They are for you and for now. Rest a moment in the knowledge that you are a deeply and relentlessly loved daughter of God.

OPEN YOUR BIBLE TO PSALM 34:18 AND ZEPHANIAH 3:17 AND COPY THE VERSES BELOW.

An extension of Christ's own ministry and commission to His disciples, the church's specialty is welcoming the outcast and being a haven to the hopeless. But sometimes we fail in our mission, forgetting to extend that same love to our spiritual brothers and sisters. We're a family of broken human beings who all need Jesus, and there are moments the church feels more like a family feud than a family of faith. But this discord among God's children isn't anything new; it is as old as the church itself.

In the context of our conversation today, I can't help but wonder: *Would this still be the case if we read and applied Scripture by God's rules instead of our own?*

OPEN YOUR BIBLE TO EPHESIANS 4:1-6.

Read how Paul describes the relationship and unity among believers, circling the word "one" every time it appears. How many times does Paul use the word "one" in this passage? Why do you think that is?

OPEN YOUR BIBLE TO ROMANS 14:19.

What are followers of Jesus called to pursue?

If our aim as the church is to promote the gospel as our one hope, then we ought to use the Scriptures not for tearing one another down, but for strengthening one another in truth and love (Eph. 4:15).

I find myself reading these passages and thinking, *Yes, let's all do that!* Building each other up sounds great, doesn't it? But agreeing is not the same as acting—we must find ways to actually and actively build one another up in the faith.

Just as God provides us with the gift of community so we don't have to walk the road of faith alone (stay tuned for more on community in Week Six!), He also provides the gift of His Word so we can walk in the way of the gospel and help others do the same.

OPEN YOUR BIBLE TO 2 TIMOTHY 3:16-17, AND READ IT ALOUD.

By now this passage should be familiar to you—Paul's words to Timothy about Scripture bear repeating! But take a closer look. Notice the applications for and results of this sword called Scripture.

What are the intended uses of Scripture? List them here.

What are the results of these appropriate uses of Scripture?

According to the true Book itself, Scripture is to be used for these things—reproof (not injury), correction (not destruction), and training (not controlling). **Applying truth responsibly means handling it in the right way and for the right purposes, for others and ourselves.**

Earlier in his second letter to Timothy, Paul writes, "Keep your attention on Jesus Christ" (2 Tim. 2:8). He summarizes the gospel, urging Timothy to focus on these most important things.

OPEN YOUR BIBLE TO 2 TIMOTHY 2:14-15.

Let's make Paul's words our prayer today, asking the Holy Spirit to help us "rightly handle the word of truth" (ESV), applying it not haphazardly but responsibly for ourselves and others.

APPLY TRUTH PERMANENTLY

"Mi sono perso."

It means "I'm lost" in Italian, and it's a handy phrase to know if ever find yourself lost in Italy. I've never been, but my friend Kaitlin spent a semester there back in college, and I love the tales of her gondola-riding, noodle-making adventures.

She tells the story of how, before she left, she imagined the day of her arrival unfolding like a scene from a movie. She would head straight from the airport to an adorable old hotel, stepping daintily into a bathtub near a stained-glass window, Italian dictionary in hand, luxuriously soaking in the language. Hours later she would emerge from the soapy suds having memorized all the words she'd need for an exciting and successful four months in a foreign land:

Ciao. Spaghetti. Bruschetta. Got it.

Before her trip, Kaitlin's Italian teacher, Francesco (because of course that was his name), lectured the class on the importance of learning basic phrases and always remembering directional terms in the language. But while Francesco lectured, Kaitlin daydreamed and doodled *"bacio"* in her journal next to a sketch of the Leaning Tower of Pisa, certain she'd pick up the words she needed once she arrived.

Sure enough, Kaitlin soon found herself lost in her new favorite city, scanning her surroundings for clues to the way home. She was lost. Everything looked unfamiliar yet somehow the same. Frantically unzipping her backpack, she pulled out the notebook from Italian class and threw it open, hoping to find the words for "right" or "left" or even her address. Nothing. Just doodles and the Italian word for "kiss." She had been given the opportunity to store everything about her destination in her heart and mind, and had missed it completely.

Can you relate to Kaitlin? Have you ever been given the opportunity to memorize something important but decided it could wait until it was urgent? Describe a time when you were lost for the right words, wishing you'd taken an earlier opportunity to prepare.

Thinking back on Kaitlin's story, I wonder, *Are you and I doing the same thing with God's Word? Do we think we're prepared for life in a "foreign land" because we sit in on a few orientation classes? Are we content to listen to the pretty-sounding words and comforting phrases, forgetting that all of Scripture is a map to the very center of our Heavenly Father's heart?*

The truth we read in quiet is far too easily forgotten as we reenter the noise and hustle of our lives. Memorizing Scripture applies God's Word to our hearts and minds permanently, giving us tangible promises and clear directions so that we might not sin against Him.

OPEN YOUR BIBLE TO FIND WHAT THE BIBLE HAS TO SAY ABOUT WRITING GOD'S WORD ON OUR HEARTS. MAKE A FEW NOTES ABOUT EACH PASSAGE.

DEUTERONOMY 6:4-9

DEUTERONOMY 11:18

JOSHUA 1:8-9

PSALM 119:9-11

PROVERBS 2:1-5

OPEN YOUR BIBLE AND READ MATTHEW 4:1-11.

When Jesus was tempted by Satan in the wilderness, what did Jesus use to combat the Devil's advances?

What happened in verse 11 after Jesus repeatedly quoted memorized Truth to Satan?

Recalling memorized Scripture isn't a party trick for the overachievers; it's a way home for the homesick. Let's invest in relief for our homesick hearts today by applying Scripture permanently. Let's store up His Words and recount His promises.

When we find ourselves lost or tempted, unsure which direction is home, may we recall the Scripture-map that takes us straight to the heart of God.

APPLY TRUTH PERMANENTLY

Because the Bible instructs us to memorize Scripture, and Jesus leads us by example, let's memorize Psalm 19:7-9 together.

7 The instruction of the Lᴏʀᴅ is perfect,

renewing one's life;

the testimony of the Lᴏʀᴅ is trustworthy,

making the inexperienced wise.

8 The precepts of the Lᴏʀᴅ are right,

making the heart glad;

the command of the Lᴏʀᴅ is radiant,

making the eyes light up.

9 The fear of the Lᴏʀᴅ is pure,

enduring forever;

the ordinances of the Lᴏʀᴅ are reliable

and altogether righteous.

TRY THESE TIPS FOR MEMORIZING SCRIPTURE:

- Write it several times in one sitting. The more you write it, the better it will stick.
- Post it in a place you visit often (above the kitchen sink, on the fridge, in your car). Try using a dry erase marker on your mirror.
- Save the verses you want to memorize as a lockscreen on your phone. (She Reads Truth provides lots of Scripture lock screens on our Bible app.)
- Sing it. If you can't find a song for the verse you're learning, make up your own!
- Write it on your arm and make it your goal to have it memorized by the time it wears off.
- Try taking a month (or a year!) to memorize a whole chapter or book of the Bible. Instead of learning lots of short verses here and there, take on a big chunk and chip away at it bit by bit.

  What are some of your favorite ways to memorize Scripture? Plan to share them with the group next time you gather.

APPLY TRUTH PRAYERFULLY

Remember those Magic Eye books from the 90s?

If you were born in the 90s or later and can't remember because you were in diapers, it's okay—consider this a mentoring moment. You're welcome.

Magic Eye books were colorful, abstract books whose sudden spike in popularity landed them a line of calendars, lunch boxes, mouse pads—even neckties. They were made with autostereograms, which allow some people to see 3D images by focusing on 2D patterns. Basically, they were a colorful bunch of random dots you could stare at for hours and see nothing. Then your buddy would walk by and say, "Hey! Cool sailboat!" and you'd be frustrated and furious all at once. *How could I not see it? How can I still not see it now that I know what I'm looking for?*

Parables, in a way, are like Magic Eye pictures. Jesus would tell 2D stories with 3D meaning, but it took help to get His hearers past simply "seeing" to actually "perceiving." It wasn't His way of guarding the secrets of the Kingdom—it was a way of revealing truth to those who believed.

OPEN YOUR BIBLE TO THE PARABLE OF THE SOWER IN MATTHEW 13.

For now, just read verses 1-9 and summarize the story in bullet points or a sketch in the space below.

OPEN YOUR BIBLE. NOW READ MATTHEW 13:10-23.

Jesus did not explain every parable He taught. In fact, He explained very few. But here, at the request of His disciples, He circles back around to give them eyes to see in 3D what they were struggling to make sense of in 2D.

Isn't that just like the kingdom of God? It has more dimensions than we can hope to grasp this side of Heaven. But the Holy Spirit isn't the buddy that laughs at how easily he can see the "sailboat" we can't see. He sits with us now like Jesus sat with His disciples then. He makes wise the simple. (That's us!) He helps us focus our eyes until we not only see, but truly *perceive and understand* the truth and beauty before us in God's Word!

Applying truth prayerfully means inviting the Holy Spirit to be our companion as we open our Bibles.

OPEN YOUR BIBLE AGAIN, KNOWING IT IS FOR YOU AND FOR NOW.

While we're in Matthew 13 learning about how Christ (and the Holy Spirit) helps us understand truths about the Kingdom, let's read the Parable of the Sower one more time, focusing this time on verses 3-9 and 18-23.

BEGIN WITH PRAYER: Using Jesus' promise in John 16:13, write a prayer asking the Holy Spirit to be your guide as you study.

NOW, ASK YOURSELF:

What type of ground do you think best represents your relationship with God's Word? Maybe you relate with more than one type of soil. Why do you think it is this way?

What might be choking the Word in your life? This could be many things—from circumstances or people, to distrust or disregard. Ask the Holy Spirit to help you truly consider this question.

What can be done to make our hearts "good soil" for the hearing AND receiving of the gospel?

Now, using the words in Hebrews 4:7, write a short prayer of response.

Let's be women who apply God's Word prayerfully.

Let's ask the Holy Spirit to give us eyes to see and ears to hear, helping us perceive in 3D things we have previously only seen in 2D.

Let's have hearts that receive the truth so that we can be made fruitful.

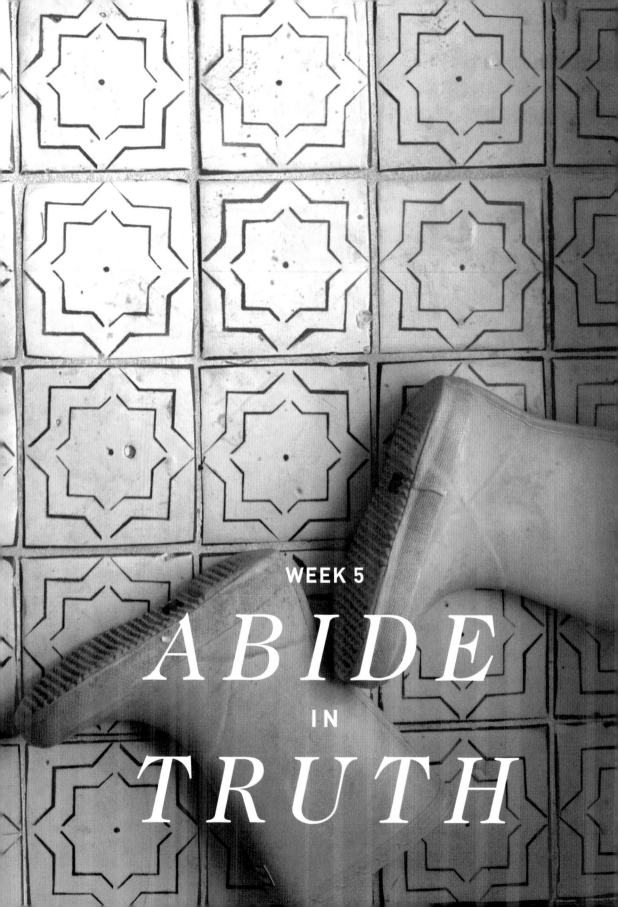

WEEK 5

ABIDE

IN

TRUTH

"She's my whole-life friend."

That's what my daughter said when she was three, pointing to a picture of her best friend who was also three. It was an accurate statement. Our best friends had welcomed their first child just three months before we welcomed our own. We have a photo of my girl in the hospital, just one day fresh, being held up next to her already-established "BFF" who was snoozing soundly in her carseat. If you think that photo must be adorable, you're right.

The term has stuck, and there are more than a handful of "whole-life friends" connected to our family. Most of mine started out as roommates in my 20-something years, those people who knew me so well they had no choice but to love me or hate me. They knew the junk food I ate. They knew how often I showered (or how often I didn't). They knew every mood I could swing and how fast I could swing it—from showtune-singing, movie-quoting Amanda, to highly-irritable, too-tired Amanda. My life friends have known me at my best and my worst. It's part of what being a life friend is all about.

The kind of abiding we humans are used to implies *familiarity*. You learn who a person is in various contexts—say, at the beach vs. at the dentist—and you learn their habits, like how they take their coffee or at what point in their morning routine they brush their teeth.

It implies *trust*. If you live with someone, you eventually have to let your guard down; it's just the way it goes. You're going to discover their terrible taste in music, and they're going to discover that you snore, and you both have to be okay with that.

While this type of abiding is good and helpful for creating a life friend, it's a faint illustration of what it means for us to abide in Christ. There is familiarity, yes. We long for an intimate knowledge of our Savior's heart! And there is trust. By walking with Him, we learn to lean on Him. But what else does it mean to abide with someone you can't see, much less share a pizza with?

When we abide in Jesus—resting, remaining, and returning by way of the cross—something happens in that invisible connection. Our hearts are stirred in the stillness. We are transformed in the quiet. And unlike that time you acquired your roommate's taste for curry—this change is wonderfully predictable: *when we abide in Jesus, we become more like Him.*

LOOKING BACK:

Last week, as we explored the tricky topic of Scripture application, we also discussed Scripture misapplication—the reality of it, effects of it, and ways to avoid it. Have you personally witnessed or experienced this type of misuse of God's Word? As tough as it is to talk about it, it is important we as a family of believers listen to and learn from one another as we seek to live out the gospel together.

Look back at the end of Week Four, Day One together. Why do you think it's so tempting to take Scripture out of context? Is there room for grace as we sincerely seek to honor God's Word by applying it appropriately and responsibly, knowing that we and others will fail at times to do that well?

On Day Three of last week, we talked about the privilege (and challenge!) of applying truth permanently to our hearts with Scripture memorization—and we asked you about your favorite ways to do just that. Do you have some fun tips and tricks for memorizing Scripture? Share them with your group!

WATCH THE VIDEO:

To hear more from Raechel and Amanda, download the optional video bundle to view Week Five at *www.lifeway.com/openyourbible.*

NOW, LET'S TALK:

OPEN YOUR BIBLE AND READ JOHN 15:1-8 ALOUD.

What two verbs does Jesus use repeatedly in this passage? Identify them together. Compare these two words in multiple Bible translations in your group.

Read verse 4 again. What is Jesus' specific command in this verse?

Now read verse 5. What is Jesus' promise to us if we obey His command?

LET'S TALK ABOUT THE WAYS IN WHICH WE CONFUSE "ABIDING" AND "PRODUCING."

According to the exercise above, which comes first, the producing or the abiding (or remaining)? How have you tried to reverse this process in your own life?

Describe a circumstance in your life when you believed that producing fruit was more urgent than abiding in the true Vine. What do you think made producing feel more important than abiding?

When we attempt to produce fruit without abiding, we disobey Jesus' command in John 15:4. What negative consequences have you witnessed that were the result of striving to produce fruit apart from abiding in Christ?

At the end of the "Start Here," Amanda asked the question, "What does abiding in Christ look like?" What do you think? What words come to mind? Discuss those as a group now.

It's a loaded question, one we'll work to answer this week. Here are the elements of abiding we'll examine together. Read them aloud to one another now.

ABIDING MEANS RESTING: to still our feet and our hearts, to stop striving and sit in the knowledge that He is God and we are not.

ABIDING MEANS REMAINING: to stay intentionally close to the Savior, to remain close to Him in His Word in each season and circumstance.

ABIDING MEANS RENEWING: to be made a new creation the first time and every time we come back to Him.

ABIDING MEANS RETURNING: to come back again and again, bringing our experiences home to Jesus in worshipful prayer.

Which of these feels the most challenging to you? Commit to praying for a member of your group this week as the Holy Spirit teaches her what it looks like to abide in Christ.

Abide in Him.

ye are the branches—
you need to be nothing more.
you need not for one
single moment of
the day take upon
you the responsibility
of the Vine.
ANDREW MURRAY

DAY ONE
REST IN TRUTH

*My mom used to wake us up
with pots and pans.*

My brother and I would be sleeping soundly in our respective rooms, ignoring our alarms and Mom's best efforts to lure us out of bed to get dressed for school. Eventually, up the stairs she'd come, banging a wooden spoon on a steel pot or metal pan or whatever was handy in the kitchen, a big grin on her face. She knew to relish moments like those.

Evidently rest was not a challenge for me when I was younger, no matter how loud life got. It came more naturally and more soundly, regularly and effectively pushing aside the activities and cares of life to make space for quiet and being.

Tack on twenty years and rest has taken on unicorn status. It is glorious and beautiful, but rare—almost fictional! When it finds me, I know it in an instant. Like when a stranger walks into a family reunion, moments of true rest are recognizable not because they are familiar but precisely because they aren't. In our days packed to the brim with running and doing and striving, pockets of rest feel out of place, making us—runners and doers and strivers that we are—feel out of sorts. It's those moments of rest that jar us awake to the good stuff, allowing our hearts to come up for air and stirring our curiosity toward God and our questions of faith.

Reflect on the idea of true rest in your own life. Why do you think rest makes us so uncomfortable? Why have we trained our adult selves to see rest as unproductive, lazy, even indulgent?

What have you prized above rest, either consciously or subconsciously?

OPEN YOUR BIBLE *AND READ MATTHEW 11:28-30.*

Rest doesn't have to take on unicorn status. Jesus promises it to us! What instructions does Jesus give for finding rest?

Speaking as the girl who still struggles to wake in the morning (though now from sleeping too little instead of too soundly), I'm uncomfortable with rest because it means loosening my grip. It means slowing my feet and temporarily, or even permanently, forfeiting my plans. Rest begs me to relinquish control—to cease striving and commence trusting. These reasons are precisely why rest is so key to our call to abide in God and His Word.

Mary of Bethany is my favorite example of a "rester" in Scripture. While her sister Martha (bless her!) was scurrying around the house, doing what needed to be done, Mary was sitting at Jesus' feet. She ceased readying her home, readying herself, she even ceased serving Jesus for the opportunity to *sit* with Jesus.

OPEN YOUR BIBLE *TO LUKE 10:38-42 AND READ THE STORY FOR YOURSELF.*

Do you see yourself more in Mary or Martha? In what ways?

What does Jesus say to Martha? See verses 41-42.

Those things Martha busied herself with were good, even commendable, but only one thing was truly necessary—to sit at the feet of the Savior. **Those other things were important, but listening to Jesus' words was urgent.**

Oh, but I am so bad at sitting! I am so reluctant to cease my striving. I am so slow to create space and quiet to meet with my God and Him alone. No distractions, no agendas, just resting at the feet of Jesus.

When I need written permission to rest in the presence of the Lord, I go to the Psalms. Those poems are like a permanent hall pass when I'm overwhelmed, a doctor's note to skip class when all my papers are overdue.

OPEN YOUR BIBLE TO PSALM 119:114. FILL IN THE BLANKS BELOW.

You are my _____ and my _____; I put my hope in Your word.

The Hebrew words here for "shelter" and "shield" mean exactly that—a covering, a defense. The psalmist runs to Scripture for cover! It is his best defense. God's Word calls us to trust Him by setting our striving aside and acknowledging Him as our haven. Psalm 91 follows suit, calling the Lord a refuge and fortress: "He will cover you with His feathers; you will take refuge under His wings" (v. 4).

Be still. Stop. Sit with me awhile, we hear the Father say. And when we do? "He gives power to the faint, and to him who has no might he increases strength" (Isa. 40:29, ESV). When we rest in Him, our rest becomes our strength.

Friends, there is nothing we can do with our efforts that our almighty God cannot do by His Word. Likewise, there is nothing you or I can do to negate the truth of His Word. We cannot make it more true, we cannot make it less true. No, our job is to rest here *in* its truth.

Andrew Murray, a prolific minister in South Africa in the 19th century, wrote an entire book about abiding. In it he says this: "Ye are the branches—You need be nothing more. You need not for one single moment of the day take upon you the responsibility of the Vine. You need not leave the place of entire dependence and unbounded confidence."[1]

Which part of this quote speaks to you most? Underline it. How does Murray's statement underscore the importance of rest as part of abiding?

Are you resting in the truth of God's Word? If not, why? If so, how? What are some other tangible ways you can abide in Christ by resting?

Tonight my mom came to visit (I haven't seen her bang any pots or pans lately, but she's still a champ at relishing). When it came time for her to leave, I watched as the taillights of her car meandered down our gravel driveway. A flicker in the distance caught my eye—countless fireflies dotting the dark treeline along the creek. They looked choreographed yet whimsical, like Christmas lights in July.

I stopped to watch, and I stayed awhile—no running, no doing, no striving. Just resting. It was one of the most beautiful and productive parts of my day.

REMAIN IN TRUTH

"You can't go home again."

There was a time when that saying didn't bother me. When I left home for college, and then left my college town for a new city, I prided myself on not looking back. I'd miss my people and our places, sure, but this was the way life was supposed to go, right? You pick up, you move on. You look with confidence toward the better things that will surely greet you.

That was then. But now? Now my ideal scenario is to buy a big, heavenly plot of land and plop all the people I love most right down on it.

I casually browse nearby real estate listings for faraway family members (who've expressed no interest in moving, but they'll come around). I regularly scheme for local job opportunities well-suited to the friends I miss. Going home is no longer something I can do without—it is something I long for, something I need.

What does "home" mean to you? When you feel the need to go home, whether that looks like certain people or a particular place, what do you do?

When I think of the people on earth who feel like home to me, I'm reminded how much greater still is the home I have in Christ. Call it cliché if you like, but it's the sweetest cliché there is. Like all those "Heroes of the Faith" in Hebrews 11, I "now desire a better place—a heavenly one" (v. 16). According to Jesus' own words in John 15, He has made His home in us and our home is found in Him!

OPEN YOUR BIBLE TO JOHN 15:1-5. WRITE VERSE 5 BELOW.

Like a branch growing out of the vine, so are the saved to the Savior.
Remaining in Him—not behind, not beside, but *in*—is the way we are meant
to live.

It sounds warm and fuzzy in theory, but what does it mean to "remain" in
practice? We are people on the move, after all, from one city to the next, from
this job to that. With passions galore and a drive to explore, we humanfolk like
to choose our own adventure—like those books my brother and I read as kids.
If life is always pushing us forward, how then do we obey Jesus' call to remain?

Yesterday we talked about Mary of Bethany, my favorite rester in the Bible.
So you won't be shocked to learn that I have a favorite remain-er, too: Mary
Magdalene. Like the other Mary, this one also clung to Jesus and His words.
But what I love most about Mary Magdalene is her continued pursuit of the
Lord, through changing landscapes and uncertain circumstances.

When we meet her, she is already following Jesus. (Later the Gospel
writers will casually mention that Jesus had cast seven demons out of her!)
Throughout His ministry, she continues to follow—sometimes close, often at
a distance, but always in earshot. Mary followed Jesus when He walked the
earth, and she even sought Him after His death.

OPEN YOUR BIBLE TO JOHN 20. READ VERSE 1, THEN VERSES 11-16.

**When does this story take place? What is Mary's reaction when she cannot
find Jesus?**

Jesus was Mary's home. She just wanted to be where He was. And so she kept
coming back—not once or twice, but for a lifetime. Times changed, but Mary
remained.

I wonder if Mary Magdalene would correct me if she knew how often I
misread that famous "abide" passage in John 15 as delivering a mandate to
fruitfulness, a command to produce. Because if I look at the passage more
closely, I see the true command is to remain:

JOHN 15:4

*Remain in Me, and I in you. Just as a branch is unable to produce fruit by itself
unless it remains on the vine, so neither can you unless you remain in Me.*

How, then, do we remain? What does it look like to abide by remaining?

OPEN YOUR BIBLE *TO THE VERSES BELOW.*

What do they teach us about what it looks like to remain? Note the instructions to stay close to Jesus, as well as what it looks like to stay close to Him.

JOHN 8:31

JOHN 10:27

JOHN 13:35

COLOSSIANS 3:2-1

There's a reason we love coming home. And there was a reason Mary Magdalene sought Jesus. Whether a physical place or loved one's embrace, the power of home is in the way it defines us and gives everything else meaning.

Friends, Jesus Christ is our home, and the Bible is where we meet Him. Remaining in truth does not simply mean being near it or visiting on occasional holidays; it means a lifetime of faithfully returning to its pages, a record of regular rest in God's Word. Like Mary Magdalene, may we relentlessly remain in the presence of our God. And may we relish our reward—the company of the risen Christ Himself.

DAY THREE
RENEWED IN TRUTH
What about "abiding" makes us new?

This week we are exploring what it means to abide in the Word of God. Once we approach it, engage it, and apply it—it's time to set a pace. It's time to make God's Word no longer "what we do" but "who we are."

Two days ago, we watched Mary of Bethany rest in stillness when the Lord came to visit, and yesterday Mary Magdalene remained in His presence, following Jesus wherever He went. We're learning that abiding in Truth is not only a *resting* stillness, it's also an *active* stillness. It is going to where Jesus is, and knowing there is nothing more urgent than a relationship with Him. It's pursuing His presence like a prize!

But as we do this—this active stillness—something is happening. "Those who hope in the LORD," Isaiah 40:31 tells us, "will renew their strength" (NIV). When we see the presence of the Lord as the prize, He will "renew a steadfast spirit" within us (Ps. 51:10). In fact, 2 Corinthians 5:17 tells us, "if anyone is in Christ, he is a new creation; old things have passed away, and look, new things have come." *But how does the renewal come? What about abiding makes us new?*

OPEN YOUR BIBLE TO JOHN 15:1-4. WE ONLY NEED TO READ TWO VERSES IN TO KNOW THAT EVERY BRANCH GETS THE ATTENTION OF THE VINEDRESSER.

What happens to the branches that do not produce fruit?

What happens to every branch that produces fruit?

Circle the word "every" above. Does that make you uncomfortable?

If you have even a little experience in gardening, you may already know pruning sometimes means cutting off lovely-yet-superfluous parts of us, to make us more solid. More fruitful. Even more beautiful.

Notice, the branches that aren't abiding are cut off (not pruned), but the fruit-bearing branches are pruned. The Vinedresser does not leave any branch untouched; but if we are *abiding*, He *renews* us! He lovingly and expertly pares us back "so that [we] will be even more fruitful" (v. 2, NIV).

OPEN YOUR BIBLE TO ISAIAH 5:1-6,
A PASSAGE CALLED "SONG OF THE VINEYARD."

Who is the owner of the vineyard?

Who does the vineyard represent?

When his well-kept vineyard doesn't produce fruit, what does the owner do (v. 6)?

If the vineyard is the people of Israel, and the owner is God, who fulfills the "Song of the Vineyard" in John 15?

After reading John 15 and Isaiah 5 together, does the act of pruning seem more or less desirable than it did? Write a prayer to that end.

Abiding in truth transforms us—it makes us new creations (2 Cor. 5:17). Paul reminds Timothy—and us—that the Bible can teach us and train us, but it will also rebuke and correct us (2 Tim. 3:16).

Pruning isn't always a removing of good for better, sometimes pruning is correcting— removing bad for good. In either case, pruning is an act of preservation.

What two promises does Jesus make in John 16:33?
Write them below.

Now read 2 Corinthians 4:7-18, paying special attention to 16-18. (We love to have you read the full section for context!) Copy those last three verses below, underlining or circling the promises.

Write a prayer in the space provided. Confess, repent, petition, and praise! With the truth you've studied about pruning in mind, pray some of the passages you've read. Ask the Father to make you a new creation, renewing you day by day.

RETURN IN PRAYER

"Pray constantly."

As one who treasures word illustrations, it's tempting to take these two words—the entirety of 1 Thessalonians 5:17—and assign an abstract comparison to make it more palatable, an illustration to make it fit more tidily into our everyday reality. But it's tough to explain away such a clear and undiluted statement: "pray constantly." Two words. That's it.

> I do love a good metaphor—they're the cotton candy to my circus—but there's no sugar-coating this command from God's Word. The verse means exactly what it says: our life is to be an ongoing prayer to the Lord. Our words and breath are a conversation with our Savior. To abide in God's Word in the ways we've discussed this week unequivocally requires our constant return to Him in prayer.
>
> **What is your reaction when you read the command to "pray constantly"? Is returning to God in prayer something you do often or wish you did?**

We may be skeptical when it comes to the instructions of this little verse, but let's not write it off as exaggeration just yet. Let's first spend some time with Scripture's resident expert on returning, a shepherd-boy king named David.

David was a seasoned wanderer, imperfectly traveling the spectrum from poetic worshiper to murderous adulterer and back again. But the Bible is filled with psalms written by our sinful, soulful brother as he continually came before his God. If "pray constantly" is the command, it seems David actually did it, and God saw fit to leave us a record of it.

David returned to God in all manner of circumstances and emotions—when he was victorious and when he failed, when he rebelled and when he obeyed, whether his life was threatened or preserved.

OPEN YOUR BIBLE TO PSALM 9:1-4.

Who is David speaking to in this psalm? What are the circumstances?

What seems to be the emotional tone of the psalm?

OPEN YOUR BIBLE TO PSALM 63:1. DAVID WROTE THIS PSALM FROM THE FIGURATIVE AND LITERAL WILDERNESS OF JUDAH.

How is its tone different from that of Psalm 9? How is it the same?

There are times we find poor David running for his life, hiding in caves from the men who want to destroy him. But when David ran, he ran to his heavenly Father. Psalm 142 is actually labeled "a Psalm of David, when he was in the cave. A prayer." "Rescue me ... they are too strong for me," he cries (v. 6). The fear in his voice progresses to sorrow in very next psalm, when we hear our wanderer groan, "My spirit is weak within me; my heart is overcome with dismay" (Ps.143:4).

Joy and sorrow, desperation and fear—all of them drove David back to God's presence.

Do you tend to pray more in some seasons than others? With 1 being the least and 5 being the most, number the seasons below according to how likely you are to pray in the midst of them.

____ *Joy* ____ *Sorrow* ____ *Fear* ____ *Triumph* ____ *Need*

There's yet another circumstance that bowed David down low, causing him to cry those trademark prayers with the kind of honesty that makes us squirm. When David was covered in the filth of his own sin—fresh from committing adultery and plotting an innocent man's death—he returned to God as the guilty man he was.

In 2 Samuel 12, Nathan, a prophet of the Lord, confronts David after his indiscretions with Bathsheba and draws out his confession. In the intensity of this moment of conviction, David pens Psalm 51, my personal go-to when the darkness of my heart is too much to articulate.

OPEN YOUR BIBLE AND READ PSALM 51:1-12.

Underline the various phrases David uses to confess his sin to the Lord.

According to verse 12, where does David want to remain?

Walking, running, crawling to the throne of the Most High God—these, too, are actions of abiding. You and I are called to turn and return with our whole heart, our whole, messed-up selves. Our actions do not give us the right to return. Our emotions do not grant us access to God. **We return because—and only because—Jesus Christ goes before us.** His cross is the path by which we return to our holy, gracious God.

OPEN YOUR BIBLE AND READ JOEL 2:12-13.

According to the prophet, what is God's response when we return to Him?

Turn to Psalm 145:18. Where is the Lord when we call out to Him?

Friends, abiding without prayer is not true abiding. Returning to the Father in prayer is our lifeline—a lifeline fueled by time spent in the pages of God's Word. From our caves of fear and desperate deserts, even from the pitch-black corners of our sinful hearts, may we learn to cry out to the only One who is mighty to save.

OPEN YOUR BIBLE BACK TO PSALM 51, AND CHOOSE SOME OR ALL OF THE VERSES TO PRAY TO THE LORD. PRACTICE RETURNING IN PRAYER AS YOU LEARN TO MORE FULLY ABIDE IN HIM.

WEEK 6

LIVE
IN
TRUTH

"You are not alone."

How often do we need to hear those words? As someone who tends toward island mode a little too often, I could stand to be reminded several times a day that I don't have to go it alone.

Do you remember the tree from Week Two? That awesome, expansive tree that was just right for 5-year-old Raechel? We said it was like the Word of God, which proved itself trustworthy and able to challenge, engage, and inspire climbers of all ages and abilities. I didn't have to worry that it wasn't for me or that I wasn't big enough. The tree—and the Bible—was approachable and worth approaching.

Well, I'm older now. (We won't say how old. *Ahem.*) And the Word of God, like the tree, has proven itself trustworthy for decades of climbing up and down and all around. And the wildly beautiful truth? Just as it was for *me* and for *then*, it is still for *me* and for *now*.

This only makes me want to keep climbing. Those branches up high, the ones that seemed dark or dangerous from down low, are where the sun shines brightest, making the leaves a near-magical display. Every branch above and beneath me looks brand new all over again. I want to climb more, but I can't do it alone. *I wasn't designed to do it alone.*

The good news is this: I'm not alone in this tree and neither are you. Not only is the Climbing Guide there with us (you guessed it—the Holy Spirit), there are other climbers in the tree. Lots of them! Some climbers are higher up than me, some are in the lower branches. We are all climbing in that tree together.

There is a sense of community under the canopy of leaves that gives me confidence to reach up to another climber for help when I can't do it on my own. And when I see someone below me struggling to make sense of the branches, I get to reach down to help them, pointing out footholds they can't see from where they stand—just like someone did for me when I was there. This community of climbers rejoices to see people get their first "boost" onto the lowest branch of the tree, and we celebrate all the more watching friends taking tentative steps toward the tree for the very first time.

This week, let's look around at each other like we're all climbers in the same tree. Let's talk about what it looks like—*really* looks like—to reach up and down. How can we help each other climb higher? Let's resolve to be on the lookout for climbers who think they're alone, and invite them to climb with us.

LOOKING BACK:

Think back to the time you spent talking about rest this week. If 1 is "I'm going all day and fall asleep mid-action at 2 a.m." and 10 is "I've carved out a rhythm of rest in my life on daily, weekly, monthly, and yearly levels," where do you most often find yourself on the able-to-rest scale? In light of today's story about the community of climbers, what can you learn from each other in this area?

When asked what you prize above rest (either consciously or subconsciously), what was your answer? Are there similarities in your group?

What truth did you learn about remaining this week? What is the Holy Spirit teaching you?

When you ranked the "seasons" in which you pray, what came out on top? On bottom? How can you encourage one another?

WATCH THE VIDEO:

To hear more from Raechel and Amanda, download the Week Six optional video at *www.lifeway.com/openyourbible.*

NOW, LET'S TALK:

In today's story, Raechel talks about the community of climbers she's found in that big tree we keep coming back to. Does the word "community" bring up any emotions for you? In what way?

Has community played a part in your relationship with God and His Word? What are some times in your life when community has bolstered you further up into the tree?

Describe a time in your life when community has been absent. How did that affect your relationship with God and His Word? Going forward, how can you attempt to prevent that experience in someone else's life?

Church and culture define community in a variety of ways. Let's see what Scripture itself has to say about community.

WHAT COMMUNITY IS...

OPEN YOUR BIBLE TO 1 CORINTHIANS 12:12-27 AND READ IT ALOUD.

Which parts of the body are most important? Are any parts of the body/ climbers in the tree unnecessary?

When you imagine the tree, do you see it as a hierarchy? How are you tempted to look at one position in the tree as more important than another?

WHAT COMMUNITY DOES...

OPEN YOUR BIBLE TO HEBREWS 10:23-25 AND READ IT ALOUD.

These three verses are so rich with instruction for what a community of believers should do. Call out each directive. Which ones look more like abiding? Which ones look more like producing?

Just as the abiding comes before the fruit in John 15, notice what instruction comes first in this list (see v. 23). What important promise comes after that first instruction?

How can we promote love and good works among each other?

How can we be concerned about one another as an overflow of the hope we have?

How should biblical community and unity affect the way we approach, engage, apply, and share God's Word?

WHO THIS COMMUNITY IS...

OPEN YOUR BIBLE A FEW VERSES BACK TO HEBREWS 10:19-22.

Look at verse 19. How did we get to be a part of this great community of believers to begin with?

The context of this passage shows a community of believers made up of both Jews and Gentiles. This was groundbreaking business at the time. If Jesus was their admission into this faith community, shouldn't this also define who is welcome in our community of faith?

As you look around the room right now, can you see each other as climbing partners? The point is not who is higher or lower in the tree—the point is that we are all in it together!

As we approach the week ahead, don't be afraid to reach out to one another to talk about what you're learning, what is challenging you, and what excites you!

We're all in this together.

We have one another only through Christ, but through Christ we do have one another.

DIETRICH BONHOEFFER

DAY ONE
REACH UP

"I'll be right there."

Those were exactly the words I needed to hear as I ended a panicked phone call to my friend Sally at 4 o'clock on a Monday afternoon. I was a newlywed and it was the new mister's first day back to work after our honeymoon. On his way out the door that morning, I promised him a great big homemade meal for supper—including his favorite, mashed potatoes. Only, once I peeled the potatoes that afternoon, I realized I had no idea what steps came next. I just knew he'd be home soon and I wanted everything to be perfect.

I'm not sure why it was so important to me that the food be hot and on the table as he walked in the door that first evening. (My standard has, let's say, "lowered" over the years.) But Sally didn't question me. She was on her way, and I knew everything would be okay.

Sally knew how to make mashed potatoes and I, it turns out, did not. So what if I was a year older than her? I knew she could help me! And that's exactly what she did. Neither of us had a ton of homemaking experience, so she was just as thrilled to help as I was to be helped. I have a photograph of that very first dinner table, a chicken main course and (I kid you not) six side dishes, plus dessert—all served on our new wedding dishes and linens. I was so proud! Not pictured was sweet Sally who slipped away just before Ryan got home.

Five years later, I still wasn't great at making mashed potatoes, but we were getting by. I made another phone call, but this time it was in the middle of the night, and it had nothing to do with root vegetables. It was the darkest night of the darkest season of my life, and I called the one person I knew had been there before me. Lisa was a woman in my church, maybe fifteen years older than me, and she answered my middle-of-the-night call.

Lisa sat up with me on the phone for over an hour that night, and more for days and months following. She knew what to do. She knew what to say and when to sit in silence. She knew how to pray. Lisa mentored me spiritually and practically, and she always took my calls.

When I needed help, I reached up. I called on someone I knew had been there before me. Now, I don't pretend that asking for help is easy. Sometimes it's super awkward or even disappointing. Sometimes no one takes your call, and you have to keep calling people until someone answers. But it's worth the trying, friend. And it's important.

Have you had a Sally or Lisa in your own life? Someone a step or fifteen ahead of you in whatever you were facing, who helped you know or do or understand what you couldn't on your own? Write about your Sally or Lisa here.

What would have happened if this person had not helped you?

Have you ever been someone else's Sally or Lisa? Did you pick up the phone when someone needed your help in a big or small way? Write about that experience here.

Are you ever tempted not to answer because of the investment of time or energy it might take? What might you miss out on by not answering the call to help?

Reaching up can and should be a constant motion of the Christian life. The Bible is for you, and it is for now, but you don't have to go it alone. Whether your struggle is simple or severe or somewhere in between, there are people all around you who have knowledge and wisdom and experience to offer—people more seasoned in their faith and more versed in the gospel.

The Christian life is personal, but it's not private—we really are in this together. God gave us the local church with "shepherds" in our pastors and elders, and "spiritual mothers" in the women who have done life a step or two (or three!) ahead of us. We can (and should) also reach beyond our immediate circles to learn from people who are not like us or who have gone before us in the church. Folks like C.H. Spurgeon, Augustine, Elisabeth Elliot, and so many others—even the stories of our own family ancestors—afford us the opportunity to reach up to men and women who lived decades or centuries before us, but treasured the same Word we have today.

For now, take some time to think on what it looks like in your own life to reach up to other tree climbers as well as explore what the Bible says about teaching, leadership, and mentoring.

What are some reasons you might reach out to another believer for help?

OPEN YOUR BIBLE: WHAT DOES SCRIPTURE SAY ABOUT "REACHING UP"?

PROVERBS 13:20

PROVERBS 27:17

HEBREWS 13:17

JAMES 5:16

Sometimes we forget to take advantage of the gospel community resources we have at our fingertips. As we close today, think of a person or two who has been a believer longer than you. Make a plan to reach up to that person before you gather as a group again.

REACH DOWN

Her name was Karen.

She saw me, and that made all the difference. I was 24, brand new to Tennessee, and 7 months pregnant with our firstborn. I don't remember feeling or looking lost, and maybe I didn't, but Karen had a radar for knowing when someone needed to be pulled in. She was the first woman to reach down to me without my asking, and I'll never forget it.

Karen reached out to me and a handful of other young women in our church, inviting us to spend Tuesday mornings in her home. She spent time preparing for our mornings together, typing out short, useful maps through the Scriptures to carry us through the hour, as well as the week ahead. Looking back, Karen was also the first person to help me understand and believe that the Bible is for me and for now. *What an enormous gift!*

Karen prayed with us. She read Scripture with us. She held our babies when they cried and provided a babysitter for the older kids in our group. We always ended our time together in her kitchen where she would comfortably and intentionally teach us things like how to stretch one roasted chicken into four meals, how to plan and plant a garden, and how to time a multi-dish meal to be hot and ready all at the same time. You know, survival training for new adults.

Karen reached down to a group of climbers on lower branches and said, *I was there once! Let me show you what I've learned.*

Hundreds of miles away from my own mother, I never knew to ask someone to teach me these things—none of us did! I didn't understand there was more to God's Word than I learned as a teenager at church and school. I didn't know I could and should read books of the Bible all the way through in one sitting, and I hadn't grasped the immeasurable value of memorized Scripture. Karen stopped her personal climb each week to reach down to us girls. She set aside one morning a week for over a year (which was a much bigger deal than I ever realized at the time!) to mentor us—all in the name of obedience and Christian community.

Reaching down is one of the most important things a Christian can do. Jesus modeled it for us His entire life. It isn't an act of condescension, judgment, or pity, and it isn't an offer based on one's faith status. It is the hand of Christ simply saying, "Let me help."

Reaching down is hospitality in its purest form. It is an invitation into our time and into our lives—even the messy parts—to show the love of Christ to others, regardless of what they have or don't have to offer.

OPEN YOUR BIBLE TO LUKE 14:13-14.

What does Jesus teach us about extending invitations?

Is there anyone you're reaching down to currently? Or, is there someone you could be reaching down to?

What have you learned in your climb that could help someone else in hers?

What has kept you from reaching down to help someone in the past? Were you worried you didn't have anything to offer? Has age or status been a roadblock? Were you concerned about what time or energy it might require?

OPEN YOUR BIBLE TO TITUS 2:3-5.

What does Paul say about women mentoring other women?

Paul uses the language "older" and "younger" when he talks about the mentoring relationship, and often age does give wisdom and perspective. But, I think "older" and "younger" can be based on more than the year we were born. Sometimes, a younger woman has been a believer longer than someone older than her.

> *Have you ever been mentored by someone younger than you? Or, have you ever mentored someone older than you? How did the Lord make that relationship fruitful?*

OPEN YOUR BIBLE AGAIN TO THE PASSAGES BELOW. WHAT DOES BIBLE HAVE TO SAY ABOUT SHARING OUR TIME, ENERGY, AND RESOURCES WITH OTHERS? MAKE NOTES AS YOU STUDY IN THE SPACE PROVIDED.

PROVERBS 22:6

ROMANS 10:15

ROMANS 12:13

2 CORINTHIANS 2:14

1 JOHN 4:21

Though the word is never used in Scripture, *mentoring* is a biblical idea. Sometimes it happened in groups, and often in one-on-one settings. Below are three of my favorite "reaching down" stories in Scripture. Read the stories and work through the questions.

JETHRO AND MOSES (EXODUS 18:1,5-27)

What was unexpected about Jethro's role as a mentor to Moses?

Moses was already an established leader of Israel when this exchange happened. What does this tell us about a leader's need for mentorship?

Why do you think this exchange was successful? What do we learn about God?

ELIZABETH AND MARY (LUKE 1:39-56)

What were some similarities and differences between Mary and Elizabeth's situations?

How important are similarities and differences in mentoring relationships?

What does this story teach us about how God uses "reaching up" and "reaching down" to prepare leaders for service?

PAUL AND TIMOTHY (1 TIMOTHY 1:1-2,12-17)

How does Paul refer to Timothy?

What is Paul telling Timothy in verses 12-16?

If you picture Paul and Timothy climbing in the tree, Paul is reaching down to Timothy, telling him how (by the grace of God) he was where he was. How do you think this strengthened Timothy's own climb?

Below are more examples of "reaching up" and "reaching down" relationships in the Bible. Look them up, read the stories, and make notes about what you're learning next to each pairing. Add any others you think of to the list.

MENTOR/MENTEE	SCRIPTURES	NOTES
Naomi & Ruth	Ruth 1:1-17	
Nathan & David	2 Samuel 12:1-15	
Elijah & Elisha	1 Kings 19:19-21	
Eli & Samuel	1 Samuel 3	
Jesus & 12 Disciples	The Gospels	
Paul & Timothy	2 Timothy 2	

LET'S PRAY. Look back on all the passages we read today about reaching down. What verse has the Holy Spirit written on your heart? What is sticking with you more than any of the others? Use that passage to pray, asking the Holy Spirit to give you boldness when it comes to encouraging others in the faith.

REMIND EACH OTHER

"You don't know me."

It's what I've felt like saying many times a well-meaning stranger has offered advice, an opinion, or even comfort into a situation I believed they couldn't possibly understand.

I remember vividly the fiasco of taking my twin babies and their toddler sister to the grocery store when they were my "3 under 3"—one hand struggling to steer our limousine-style double stroller through the dairy section and the other pulling a shopping cart full of groceries. I have a picture of one such instance, because what's a tired mama to do besides seek sympathy and solidarity via social media? The concerned glances and jolly offerings of "Enjoy every minute!" from folks at the checkout gave me hope for the moment, but they were no substitute for words of love and wisdom from the people who knew me best.

One of our designated safe places back then was the neighborhood playground. It was small and completely enclosed, affording me the luxury of sitting still awhile as the kids ran and crawled and ate mulch. Sometimes my friend Lisa would be there, too, and she'd occupy the seat next to me on the wooden bench under the tree. "You're doing a great job, mama," she would say, eyes locked on mine and holding more kindness than pity. She knew us well and she saw what I did—that this new phase of life was pure (and sometimes literal) insanity, but it was also a whole lot of lovely. "Thank you," I would sigh in relief. I always knew she meant her words, and she always knew I meant mine.

Outside the gates of community, well-meaning words can feel spoken *at* you instead of *to* you. Even true words can feel less like lifelines and more like grenades plucked from their context and tossed your way. But undergirded by gospel-believing community, truth spoken even in passing acts as a buoy, bringing our sinking hopes back to the surface. Scripture arriving via text message in the middle of a long and lousy day can feel like a wave of sweet relief, a reminder that you don't stand alone on the shore.

And is there anything more beautiful than reminding one another of the truth?

OPEN YOUR BIBLE TO EPHESIANS 5:18-21.

> **According to verse 19, how should we speak to our brothers and sisters in the faith?**

As a family of believers, we should be in the habit of speaking the gospel to each other. (I happen to be obsessed with hymns, so don't be scared if I burst into a rendition of "Great Is Thy Faithfulness" next time I hug you.) We are part of a household of faith who stands on common ground at the foot of the cross, connected across countries and cultures by the indwelling of the Holy Spirit. **It is our job and our joy to remind each other of what is true.**

OPEN YOUR BIBLE TO 2 PETER 1:12-15.

> **Is the writer of this letter delivering new information to its recipients or reminding them of what they already know?**

> **According to the second half of verse 13, what is the reminder intended to do?**

> **Why is it important to the writer to reiterate these gospel truths?**

One of the sweetest gospel-reminding moments I've ever experienced came not long ago, when a dear sister in the Lord walked in the door, war-torn and weary from the battles she's facing. "I don't know if I can do it," she said through story-filled tears. "I just don't know what to do. Can you pray for me?" And I did. I prayed "for I know that my redeemer lives," from Job 19:25 (ESV), and "behold, I am with you always," from Matthew 28:20 (ESV). I prayed promises and trust, hope and peace. They were truths she already knew, but it was my place and privilege to pray them over her when she could not find the strength to remember them on her own.

According to verse 23, why can we hold onto our hope?

The writer names a specific place in which we should remind each other of truth. What is it?

What are we to do as we await the coming of our Savior (v. 25)?

When we invest our time in one other—gathering at dinner tables and prayer circles, meeting in homes and hospital rooms—our words begin to take on the weight of shared experience, of common laughter and tears. Our reminders carry the weight of community, and worn-out clichés regain their meaning.

My sister in Christ, I can't abide for you. Nor can you abide for me. But I can encourage you to press on, and you can remind me what is true. And when life issues a sudden downpour, we can have hard conversations under the wide umbrella of grace. In the words of 2 Peter 1:13, let's commit to waking each other up with reminders of the truth, giving thanks for it together.

CLOSE YOUR BIBLE

"Close your Bible."

It's a phrase not often found in a Bible study curriculum. Or spoken from a pulpit. Or handwritten in a note from a concerned friend. Honestly, is it even appropriate to say?

The truth I have come to firmly believe is this: *Sometimes, the very best thing a Christian can do is to close her Bible and do what it says.*

I spend a lot of time behind a desk reading my Bible, reading books about the Bible, and writing books about the Bible. (Like this one. What a privilege!) So much time, in fact, that I missed an entire season of my close friend being so sick from Lyme disease that she couldn't get out of bed. She had to come to my office to see me (and bring me a bag of gummy bears) if she had any hope of getting facetime with ol' Raechel.

You guys. I was too busy reading my Bible to go visit my sick friend.

Sure, it's different for me. It's my job as a leader of a Bible-reading community to spend lots time reading the Bible. But there's a heart-truth here that I can't escape—and I bet I'm not alone. **Sometimes I'm more comfortable living in the pages of Scripture than living them out.**

But do you know what God's Word says about our faith and our actions?

OPEN YOUR BIBLE TO READ JAMES 2:14-26.

When was the last time you responded to an obvious need like the person described in verses 15-16?

What two examples does James give of Old Testament faith heroes who were justified by their faith?

James is calling us to express our faith through works. Does his charge imply that the saving work of Christ is dependent on us?

Martin Luther insisted that "saving faith" is a "living faith." What does this mean to you? What relationship do you see between the two?

I've puzzled over the faith/works conundrum on paper until I was blue in the face. Honestly, I think I've made it far more complicated in my mind than it truly is. In the end, I've found if I just lift my head, get up out of my chair, and truly see the world with the eyes of Christ, the cloudiness of it all just sort of disappears. **When I see the world as Christ sees it, I am moved to service, love, and action.**

Works are the outward obedience to an internal faith.

Think of it this way: A person is sick, so they go to the doctor they trust for a diagnosis. They have faith in the doctor's ability to care for and cure them. But when the doctor hands them their prescription slip, they gratefully tuck it into their shirt pocket and shake the doctor's hand, thanking him for his care and instruction. But they never get the prescription filled.

All too often this is me. (And maybe you, too?) I trust the Lord to search me and know me. I invite Him to teach me and rebuke me. But when He sends me out to take a step of obedience, I'd rather come back for a second opinion than do the thing He's telling me to do.

OPEN YOUR BIBLE TO THE PASSAGES BELOW.

> *If we have indeed been faithfully opening our Bibles, then we have most certainly been commissioned by its words to "close our Bible" and live out its truth. Read the passages below, making a note of the "prescription" after each verse.*

ROMANS 12:10

GALATIANS 6:2

GALATIANS 6:9-10

1 JOHN 3:17-18

OPEN YOUR BIBLE TO MATTHEW 25:40, ONE OF MY FAVORITE "CLOSE YOUR BIBLE" PASSAGES.

What does Jesus tell the crowd? Copy the verse in the space below.

James 1:22 instructs us to "be doers of the word, and not hearers only." *Doing* can be messy and difficult. We will feel broken and ill-equipped. Even still, *our lives are to be tangible reflections of the gospel—not because of who we are and what we do, but because of who He is and what He's done.* By His Spirit and in His Word, we are given all the tools our tool belt could ever hold! Living out Truth is our job, but it is our Father's work.

OPEN YOUR BIBLE TO HEBREWS 11—A WHOLE CHAPTER OF THE BIBLE DEDICATED TO THE "HEROES OF FAITH."

We do not close our Bibles because we don't need them or because we've arrived. We close our Bibles because God's Word is meant to be lived in and lived out. Take your time reading through verses 1-31, making a note of each hero's faithfulness next to their name in the chart.

Abel	*Offered to God a better sacrifice than Cain did.*
Enoch	
Noah	
Abraham	
Sarah	

Abraham (again)	
Isaac	
Jacob	
Joseph	
Moses' parents	
Moses	
Israelites	
Rahab	

Closing your Bible does not mean leaving it behind—just the opposite! When we close our Bibles and go about our days, if we are abiding in Christ, we go forward as renewed women. We take God's Word with us, written on our hearts as memorized Scripture—a map to the Father's heart as we navigate a foreign land, with the Holy Spirit as our guide.

Finish reading Hebrews 11:32-40. Reflect on its words. End your time of study by praying the words of Psalm 138:8:

"The Lord will fulfill His purpose for me. Lord, Your love is eternal; do not abandon the work of Your hands."

SHARE TRUTH

Where do we go from here?

The last week of a Bible study can feel a lot like the last week of camp. We're revived! We're filled up! We're sad to go but excited to try out our new selves on our old stomping grounds. And like camp, those who are sending us on pray more fervently than we may ever realize that we would take the things we've learned and live them—and in living them, share them.

If your affection for God and His Word has deepened in the past six weeks, if you feel more equipped or less afraid, if your appetite for special revelation has been both satisfied and amplified at the same time—this is the work of the Holy Spirit. This is *good news*—news so good we don't dare keep it to ourselves.

We believe God's Word is not just for you, not just for us, but for each and every woman.

Remember the "Invitation" section in the middle of this book? We asked you to begin considering what it might look like to share what you're learning with someone else. If this *Open Your Bible* study has knocked down walls for you and served as a fresh invitation for you to open your own Bible, what would it look like to offer that same invitation to another person?

Maybe you love big groups. Consider assembling a new group of women in your home or church and leading them through the study you've just completed.

Maybe you are a one-on-one person. Chances are, you're not alone. Someone who would never accept an invitation to join a big group would love a weekly coffee date with you. Would you reach down in the tree and offer your time?

Whether you walk through the study with a group around your dining room table, or via text message with a few friends from around the country, or in a private Facebook group of friends whose schedules make in-person meetings tough—you can be a catalyst the Holy Spirit uses to invite others into God's Word. *What a fantastic privilege.*

Friends, the Bible is for you and it is for now. But it is not about you—it is about God! It is about His steadfast love for His people. It is about His plan, His grace, His glory. And you are meant to read it. The Bible is God's special revelation to His people. Find Him right where you are when you open your Bible, and invite others to come along.

LOOKING BACK:

Last week we talked about people in our lives whom we've had the privilege of reaching up to for help—in our walk with Jesus, our understanding of Scripture, or just life itself. Share with the group a person who has been your Sally or Lisa, someone you could call on for help, prayer, and godly wisdom.

Why do you think we often hesitate to reach down in the tree and help others up? What is the value of reaching down? Do you believe everyone has someone they could reach down to in some way?

What was your response when you saw the title for the last day of the week: "Close your Bible"? In that day Raechel confessed, "Sometimes I'm more comfortable living in the pages of Scripture than living them out." Does that resonate with you? In what way?

WATCH THE VIDEO:

To hear more from Raechel and Amanda, download the optional video bundle to view Week Seven at *www.lifeway.com/openyourbible.*

NOW, LET'S TALK:

How have you been challenged over the past six weeks?

When you began this study, what words were you using to describe your relationship with God's Word? Have those words changed? What words would you use now?

How are you going to answer the invitation to share what you've learned over the last six weeks?

OPEN YOUR BIBLE TO 2 TIMOTHY 3:14-17, AND LET'S READ PAUL'S WORDS ONCE MORE.

What part of this passage stands out most to you after spending these last several weeks opening your Bibles together?

What promises do you take with you as you leave today?

Remember that prayer we prayed in Week One? Let's pray it again together as we close this study.

We are hungry for Your Word, but we don't always know where to begin.

Will You help us?

Father, we come to You confessing our inadequacy.

We need Your grace.

Holy Spirit, be our comfort and our guide.

Draw us into the pages of Scripture and reveal Yourself to us there.

Give us hearts that want to open our Bibles first in all things.

Amen.

BENEDICTION

May you go in His power, rooted in His love, with the knowledge that He is at work in and around you:

> For this reason I bow my knees before the Father, from whom every family in heaven and on earth is named, that according to the riches of his glory he may grant you to be strengthened with power through his Spirit in your inner being, so that Christ may dwell in your hearts through faith—that you, being rooted and grounded in love, may have strength to comprehend with all the saints what is the breadth and length and height and depth, and to know the love of Christ that surpasses knowledge, that you may be filled with all the fullness of God.
>
> Now to him who is able to do far more abundantly than all that we ask or think, according to the power at work within us, to him be glory in the church and in Christ Jesus throughout all generations, forever and ever.
>
> Amen.

EPHESIANS 3:14-21, ESV

START A TOOLBOX
FOR OPENING YOUR BIBLE

As you can, begin to build a Bible study toolbox of resources to enhance your understanding of the Bible. A good study Bible in an understandable translation is essential. In choosing a Bible translation, look for one that uses the earliest and most reliable Hebrew and Greek manuscripts. Some translations seek to approximate word-for-word correspondence with the Hebrew or Greek text while others seek to capture the sense of the author's intended meaning in highly readable language.[1] Other helpful tools are a concordance and Bible dictionary.

Here are features of each Bible study tool to enhance your study:

BIBLE ATLAS—Maps, charts, and photographs that illustrate the land, sites, and archaeology of the ancient world of the Bible

BIBLE DICTIONARY—Alphabetical list of key terms, places, people, events, and concepts in the Bible

BIBLE ENCYCLOPEDIA—Articles about Bible characters, events, and places, including history, religious environment, culture, language, and literature, as well as cross-references to related Scripture verses

BIBLE HANDBOOK—Brief commentary, maps, historical background, archaeological background, kings, genealogies, and other information about the Bible.

BIBLE COMMENTARY—Detailed theological analysis of specific verses and passages of Scripture. Includes a background introductory section for each book of the Bible, followed by detailed commentary of Scripture verse by verse

BIBLE CONCORDANCE—Alphabetical index of important words in Scripture and the references of texts in which they are found

TOPICAL BIBLE—Bible references to topics addressed or mentioned in the Bible

ONLINE RESOURCES—The website *www.mystudybible.com* offers free online tools for reading and studying the Bible.[2] And, of course, be sure to join the She Reads Truth online community!

BOOKS & LITERARY GENRES IN THE BIBLE

The Bible contains different genres, or literary styles, employed by its writers to convey its divinely inspired message. Knowing the type of literature we're reading helps us understand how to read it. While genres may vary within a single book, this list will give you a basic framework from which to begin a deeper dive into Scripture.

LAW

The books of Law present the individual laws given to Israel as well as the Law as a whole, or the standard by which God's people were to live and worship under the Old Covenant.

Read the Law understanding that today, we are under the New Covenant. The Law is not void; rather, it is fulfilled in Christ.

Genesis
Exodus
Leviticus
Numbers
Deuteronomy

HISTORY

The books of History present the true account of Israel from the settlement of the promised land through the destruction of Jerusalem.

Read books of History understanding they are stories of imperfect people with imperfect actions, collectively pointing us to the greater story of the gospel of Christ.

Joshua
Judges
Ruth
1 Samuel
2 Samuel
1 Kings
2 Kings
1 Chronicles
2 Chronicles
Ezra
Nehemiah
Esther

WISDOM & POETRY

The books of Wisdom present common sense sayings and philosophical reflections, while books of Poetry are lyrical writings of prayer and worship that often use metaphor and repetition.

Read books of Wisdom as a collection with a unified message, rather than precise statements. Read books of Poetry understanding they are words spoken to and about God, yet also inspired by God.

Job
Psalms
Proverbs
Ecclesiastes
Song of Songs

MAJOR & MINOR PROPHETS

The books of Prophecy present messages from God to the people living in the time of the prophet.

Read books of Prophecy understanding the historical context in which they were written and keeping in mind the big picture of God's faithful covenant to an unfaithful people.

Isaiah
Jeremiah
Lamentations
Ezekiel
Daniel
Hosea
Joel
Amos
Obadiah
Jonah
Micah
Nahum
Habakkuk
Zephaniah
Haggai
Zechariah
Malachi

GOSPELS

The Gospels present the life and teachings of Jesus Christ and contain narratives (stories), parables (illustrations), and exhortations (sayings).

Read the Gospels understanding they are the good news of the life, death, and resurrection of Jesus Christ.

Matthew
Mark
Luke
John

CHURCH HISTORY

The Book of Acts gives the history of the early church, from Jesus' ascension to Paul's ministry at Rome.

Read Acts to learn more about Paul and Peter and the work of the Holy Spirit to spread the message of our resurrected Savior and Lord.

Acts

LETTERS

The Letters, or Epistles, were written in response to a specific need or circumstance.

Read the Letters understanding the historical and spiritual context in which they were written, making sure to read each letter as a whole for the most complete understanding.

Romans
1 Corinthians
2 Corinthians
Galatians
Ephesians
Philippians
Colossians
1 Thessalonians
2 Thessalonians
1 Timothy
2 Timothy
Titus
Philemon
Hebrews
James
1 Peter
2 Peter
1 John
2 John
3 John
Jude

PROPHECY

The Book of Revelation is a combination of prophecy, apocalyptic literature, and letter written by the apostle John based on revelations from God.

Read this complex book with humility, understanding that it, too, points to the gospel and reveals Jesus Christ as King of kings, the Alpha and the Omega.

Revelation

TIMELINE

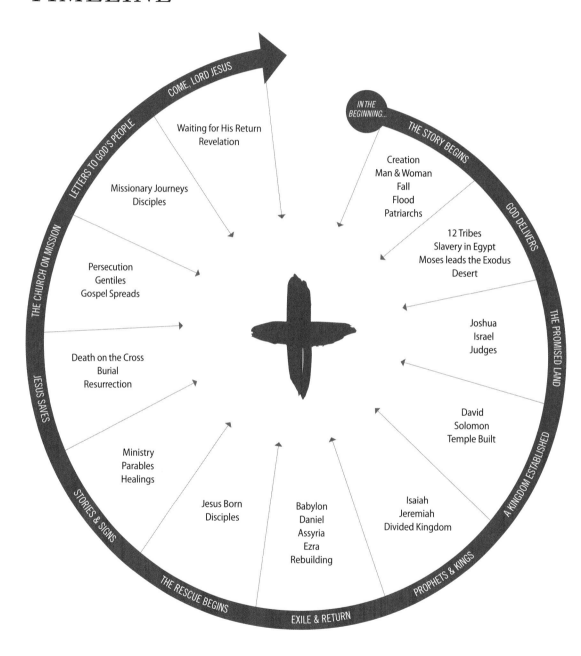

IN THE BEGINNING...

THE STORY BEGINS

Creation
Man & Woman
Fall
Flood
Patriarchs

GOD DELIVERS

12 Tribes
Slavery in Egypt
Moses leads the Exodus
Desert

THE PROMISED LAND

Joshua
Israel
Judges

A KINGDOM ESTABLISHED

David
Solomon
Temple Built

PROPHETS & KINGS

Isaiah
Jeremiah
Divided Kingdom

EXILE & RETURN

Babylon
Daniel
Assyria
Ezra
Rebuilding

THE RESCUE BEGINS

Jesus Born
Disciples

STORIES & SIGNS

Ministry
Parables
Healings

JESUS SAVES

Death on the Cross
Burial
Resurrection

THE CHURCH ON MISSION

Persecution
Gentiles
Gospel Spreads

LETTERS TO GOD'S PEOPLE

Missionary Journeys
Disciples

COME, LORD JESUS

Waiting for His Return
Revelation

CONTINUE IN BIBLE STUDY

Perhaps you are new to Bible study and have questions about the best way to learn more. Hopefully, you have fallen in love with Scripture during this study and want to dig in further.

Similar Bible studies keep you connected to believers who are learning from God's Word, too. They provide you a specific time and place to focus on some aspect of the Bible and its application to life. However, nothing compares to a daily personal encounter with God. Here are some reasons and benefits. We study the Bible to:

- Know the truth. We want to think clearly about what God says is true and valuable (see 2 Pet. 1:20-21).

- Know God in a personal relationship (see 1 Cor. 1:21; Gal. 4:8-9; 1 Tim. 4:16).

- Live well for God in this world. Living out His will expresses our love for Him (see John 14:23-24; Rom. 12:2; 1 Thess. 4:1-8; 2 Tim. 3:16-17).

- Experience God's freedom, grace, peace, hope, and joy (see Ps. 119:111; John 8:32; Rom. 15:4; 2 Pet. 1:2).

- Grow spiritually as we reject conformity to the world and are changed by the renewing of our minds (see Rom. 12:2; 1 Pet. 2:1-2).

- Minister to other Christ-followers and to those who have yet to respond to the gospel (see Josh. 1:8; 2 Tim. 2:15; 3:16-17; Eph. 6:11-17; 2 Pet. 2:1-2).

- Guard ourselves from sin and error (see Eph. 6:11-17; 2 Pet. 2:1-2).

- Build up as a Christian community with others in the body of Christ (see Acts 20:32; Eph. 4:14-16).[3]

As you open your Bible, we invite you to join the She Reads Truth online community. (We're in this together!) Find us on Twitter, Instagram, and Facebook and download the She Reads Truth Bible and Devotional app. Join the current community reading plan and share what you're learning! Use the hashtag #shereadstruth to encourage and be encouraged by other women who—just like you—are seeking to know God more through His Word.

GLOSSARY OF TERMS

ATONEMENT: Biblical doctrine that God has reconciled sinners to Himself through the sacrificial work of Jesus Christ. The concept of atonement spans both Testaments, everywhere pointing to the death, burial, and resurrection of Jesus for the sins of the world.

ATTRIBUTE: When referring to an attribute of God, it is a quality, characteristic, or property belonging to Him from the beginning of time.

GENERAL REVELATION: General Revelation is general both in its availability to all persons at all times and in its less specific content. It consists of God's self-manifestation through nature, history, and in the human personality.

IMMUTABLE: Unchanging through time; unalterable; ageless.

INERRANCY: The term describing Scripture as free from errors. The Bible is truth; Scripture is final and authoritative (Matt. 4:4,7,10; John 10:35) because it is the inspired Word of God.

INFALLIBLE: Absolutely trustworthy or sure.

INSPIRATION: The Holy Spirit's activity of directing and guiding the writers of Scripture so that "all Scripture is inspired by God" (2 Tim. 3:16). Although Scripture is inspiring to read and the authors were inspired to write; Scripture's origin means it is the very Word of God.

JUSTIFICATION: Divine, forensic act of God, based on the work of Christ upon the cross, whereby a sinner is pronounced righteous by the imputation of the righteousness of Christ.

SOVEREIGN: Biblical teaching that God possesses all power and is the ruler of all things (Ps. 135:6; Dan. 4:34-35). God rules and works according to His eternal purpose, even through events that seem to contradict or oppose His rule.

SPECIAL REVELATION: Special Revelation is primarily redemptive and personal. God communicates directly to us through His Word, His acts, and His Son in order to convey a more complete message about who He is and how He is working in the world.

REDEMPTION: The act of redeeming or atoning for a fault, mistake, or guilt, or the state of being redeemed. Deliverance and rescue from sin. Paying off sin and repurchased for God.

RIGHTEOUSNESS: Righteousness itself is grounded in the character of God. He is righteous, His law is righteous, and He alone credits righteousness to man through Jesus Christ.

Definitions adapted from Holman Bible Handbook (Nashville: Holman Bible Publishers, 1992) and Holman Illustrated Bible Dictionary (Nashville: Holman Bible Publishers, 2003).

DEEPER READING

Some of you may have lingering doubts about the total trustworthiness of the Bible. We acknowledge that and encourage you to lean in, prayerfully seeking the Lord and the council of godly men and women as you dig deeper to determine what you believe and why. If you're wrestling with the authority of Scripture, here are some resources we recommend:

The Doctrine of the Word of God by **John Frame**—One of the best "one stop shop" books when it comes to the doctrine of Scripture. It's not easy, but not too hard either. Certainly for the person who wants to go further than the basics and wrestle with significant questions about understanding the nature of the Scripture.

Taking God at His Word by **Kevin DeYoung**—A book we discovered about halfway through writing *Open Your Bible*. We found ourselves doing a lot of underlining and head nodding as we read this one. It's a great introductory book on the nature of Scripture, easy to read and very approachable. Highly recommended for the person wading into the basic questions.

The Inspiration and Authority of the Bible by **B.B. Warfield**—An old classic on the topic of Scripture from one of the greatest theologians of the 19th century. It's heavy plodding, but for those who make the journey through it, you're rewarded with rich with biblical and theological insight about the nature of the Word of God.

"Fundamentalism" and the Word of God by **J.I. Packer**—A bit of a strange title, but one of the most helpful of all the books in this list. It's brief but offers clear and concise on terminology with strong rational and commonsense defenses of the Scripture. A great book for those interested in the "battle for the Bible" debates of the last century.

Thy Word Is Truth by **E.J. Young**—A little newer and easier to digest than Warfield's magnum opus, but just as scholarly. It does a good job of unpacking the debates of the 20th century surrounding the Bible and gives a thorough treatment of the extent of biblical inspiration, defending traditional views of the Bible's authority. Another good choice for the skeptical thinker!

METHODS OF BIBLE STUDY

THE DEVOTIONAL METHOD. Prayerfully meditate on a passage, asking the Holy Spirit for understanding and application to your own life.

THE CHAPTER SUMMARY METHOD. Read a chapter of a Bible book repeatedly and then summarize the central thoughts you find in it.

THE BIOGRAPHICAL METHOD. Select a person in the Bible and research all the verses about that person in order to study his or her life and characteristics. Make notes on attitudes, strengths, and weaknesses, and look for the way .

THE TOPICAL METHOD. Collect and compare all the verses you can find on a particular topic.

THE WORD STUDY METHOD. Study important words of the Bible. How many times does a word occur in Scripture? How is it used? Find out the original meaning of the word.

THE BOOK SURVEY METHOD. Read an entire book of the Bible through several times. Study the book's background and make notes on its contents.

THE VERSE-BY- VERSE ANALYSIS METHOD. Choose one passage of Scripture. Examine it in detail by asking questions, finding cross-references, and paraphrasing each verse.

THE CHAPTER ANALYSIS METHOD. Analyze a chapter of the Bible by pouring over it verse by verse—word by word—observing every detail.

THE BOOK SYNTHESIS METHOD. After reading a book of the Bible several times, summarize the main themes and make an outline of the book.[4]

OPEN YOUR BIBLE LEADER GUIDE

The following suggestions can give you ideas for leading an *Open Your Bible* study group. The point of a group study is to support each other as you read God's Word and apply it to your lives. Take the suggestions as a place to start, but pray and complete your own study. Since every group is different, and since you have unique strengths and weaknesses, combine these suggestions with your creativity to find the best way to conduct a group.

PROMOTING THE GROUP STUDY

Promote the group through church bulletin announcements, posters, community announcements, social media, and personal invitation. At *www.lifeway.com/openyourbible* you will find downloadable promotional materials.

A SEVEN-WEEK GROUP PLAN

The suggested plan is for a seven-session group experience. However, you may custom design the group experience to fit the needs of your group or church. Distribute books and instruct group members to read through the first chapter, especially the "Start Here," before the first session, taking time to process each question. Then, for each session, the group will work as follows:

Start Here: Encourage your group to read the "Start Here" on their own before each group session. At the beginning of each session, summarize the "Start Here" as a refresher or for those who may not have read it.

Looking Back: Discuss the provided "Looking Back" questions as you begin your group discussion. These questions review what your group has learned in the previous week.

Video: To hear more from Raechel and Amanda, download the optional digital bundle videos for each week at *www.lifeway.com/openyourbible*.

Now, Let's Talk: Discuss the provided questions with your group. Encourage each group member to participate in the discussion.

BEFORE EACH GROUP SESSION

Work through the material you will cover in your next group time. Make notes of anything your group may need to further clarify. After the introductory week, complete the questions in the Bible study book for the next discussion. As you read, select the questions you believe your group will want to discuss. Draw from the questions posed throughout this Bible study. Pray about what goals the session most needs to meet for your group, and plan your session to accomplish those goals.

Remain open to the Spirit's leadership. Sometimes a group member will come with a concern or question that will result in a wonderful group experience that will bless the entire group. Other times you may need to avoid letting someone hijack the group into side issues. Experience and reliance on the Spirit will help you know the difference.

You won't get it right every time, but don't worry. If the group members are getting into the material, praying, and studying Scripture, your obedience in leadership will bear fruit!

HOW TO LEAD A BIBLE STUDY

Whether you are just starting a Bible study or continuing to grow groups in your church, we are so grateful for your investment in the lives of women. Thanks for choosing LifeWay studies, and specifically, *Open Your Bible* by Raechel Myers and Amanda Bible Williams. This study can be used in a variety of settings, including your church, home, office, or favorite coffee shop. So where do you begin?

PRAY, PRAY, PRAY. As you prepare to lead this Bible study, know that prayer is essential. Spend time asking God to work in the hearts and lives of women who will participate in the study. Begin now learning what issues the women are facing and praying about what will help them grow spiritually. Continue to pray throughout the study and encourage the women to include prayer as a daily spiritual discipline. Ask God to lead you to the women that He has called to help lead your group.

TALK TO YOUR PASTOR OR CHURCH LEADER. Ask for their input, prayers, and support.

SECURE YOUR LOCATION. Think about the number of women you can accommodate in the designated location. Reserve any tables, chairs, or needed media equipment for watching the optional videos from Raechel and Amanda at *www.lifeway.com/openyourbible*.

PROVIDE CHILDCARE. If you are inviting moms of young children or single moms, this is essential!

PROVIDE RESOURCES. Order the needed number of Bible study books. You might get a few extra for last minute drop-ins.

PLAN AND PREPARE. Become familiar with the Bible study. Preview the videos at *www.lifeway.com/openyourbible*. Prepare the outline you will follow based on the leader materials available. Go to *www.lifeway.com* to find free extra leader resources.

LEAD. One of the best things you can do as the leader is set the pace for this study. Be consistent and trustworthy. Encourage the women to follow through on the study, to attend the group sessions, and hold one another accountable to do their reading between sessions. Accept women where they are but also set expectations that motivate commitment. Listen carefully and be responsible with the discussions and sharing within the group. Keep confidences shared within the group. Be honest and vulnerable with the group and share what God is teaching you. Most women will follow your lead and be more willing to share and participate when they see your example.

FOLLOW UP BETWEEN SESSIONS. Throughout the study, stay engaged with the women in your group. Use social media, emails, or even a quick note in the mail to connect with other and share prayer needs. Let them know when you are praying specifically for them.

CELEBRATE AND SHARE. As a group, share what God is teaching you. Use #SRTOpenYourBible on social media to connect with other women doing the study.

EVALUATE. What went well? What could be improved upon? How did the women in your group respond?

NEXT STEPS. Even after the study concludes, follow up with the women in your group. You may even provide additional opportunities for them to connect with other Bible openers.

Thank you again for inviting other women to open their Bibles together! We praise the Lord for you.

ENDNOTES

INTRODUCTION

1. Timothy Keller, *The Meaning of Marriage* (New York, NY: Riverhead Books, 2013), 32.

WEEK 1

Quote from page 16: R.C. Sproul, *Knowing Scripture* (Downers Grove, IL: InterVarsity Press, 2009), 17.

1. Kevin DeYoung, *Taking God at His Word: Why the Bible Is Knowable, Necessary, and Enough, and What That Means for You and Me* (Wheaton, IL: Crossway Books, 2014), 42.

2. Matthew Henry, *An Exposition of the Old and New Testaments*. In Six Volumes, volume 6 (Edinburgh: Bell and Bradfute, J. Dickson, and J. McCliesh, 1791), 749.

3. Charles H. Spurgeon, *The Devotional Classics of C. H. Spurgeon* (Shallotte, NC: Sovereign Grace Publishers, 2008), August 27.

WEEK 2

Quote from page 38: J.I. Packer, *18 Words: The Most Important Words You Will Ever Know* (Ross-Shire, Scotland: Christian Focus Publications, Ltd., 2007), 38.

1. "Reverence," *Dictionary.com* (online), cited 19 August 2015. Available on the Internet: *dictionary.com*.

WEEK 3

Quote from page 58: Charles Spurgeon, as quoted by Jim Elliff, "My Preferred Way to Read the Bible," *Christian Communications Worldwide* (online), cited 19 August 2015. Available on the Internet: *ccwtoday.org*.

WEEK 4

Quote on page 82: Robert Murray M'Cheyne, as quoted by Andrew A. Bonar, *Memoir and Remains of the Rev. Robert Murray M'Cheyne, Minister of St. Peter's Church, Dundee* (London: William Middleton, 1845), 254.

1. Gordon D. Fee and Douglas Stuart, *How to Read the Bible for All Its Worth* (Grand Rapids, MI: Zondervan, 2014), 88.

WEEK 5

Quote from page 104: Andrew Murray, *The True Vine* (Chicago, IL: Moody Publishers, 2007), 64.

1. Ibid.

WEEK 6

Quote on page 124:Dietrich Bonhoeffer, *Life Together and Prayerbook of the Bible, Dietrich Bonhoeffer Works,* Volume 5 (Minneapolis, MN: First Fortress Press, 2005), 34.

APPENDICES

1. Adapted from *Read the Bible for Life Leader Kit.* Item 005253507. Published by LifeWay Press®. © 2010 George H. Guthrie. Made in the USA. Reproduction rights granted.

2. George H. Guthrie, *Read the Bible for Life* (Nashville: LifeWay Press, 2010), 16.

3. Ibid., 23.

4. Adapted from Rick Warren's *Bible Study Methods* (Grand Rapids: Zondervan, 2006).